"Let the same mind be in you that was in Christ Jesus. . . ."

Philippians 2:5

I do not seek to understand that I may believe,
but I believe in order to understand. For this I believe —
that unless I believe, I should not understand.

Anselm, *Proslogion*

ENGAGING GOD'S WORLD

A Reformed Vision of
Faith, Learning, and Living

■ ■ ■ ■ ■

CORNELIUS PLANTINGA JR.

William B. Eerdmans Publishing Company
Grand Rapids, Michigan / Cambridge, U.K.

Wm. B. Eerdmans Publishing Co.
2140 Oak Industrial Drive N.E., Grand Rapids, Michigan 49505 /
P.O. Box 163, Cambridge CB3 9PU U.K.
www.eerdmans.com

Printed in the United States of America

13 12 11 10 09   11 10 9 8 7

ISBN 978-0-8028-3982-4

The epigraph from Anselm is from his *Proslogion,* Chapter I: Exhortation of the Mind to the Contemplation of God (trans. Sidney Norton Deane [Chicago: The Open Court Publishing Co., 1926], 3).

Unless otherwise noted, the Scripture quotations in this publication are from the New Revised Standard Version of the Bible, copyright © 1989 by the Division of Christian Education of the National Council of Churches of Christ in the U.S.A., and used by permission.

To William Spoelhof,
President of Calvin College
(1951-76),
who led a whole community
to strive first for the kingdom of God

our citizenship in the kingdom of God, none is more obvious than becoming an active member of our local church.

Even if the Christian church is a primary instrument of the kingdom on earth, God also uses an array of other organizations to help the cause of the kingdom, each in its own sphere of influence. God uses national, intermediate, and local government to keep order and protect freedom — not an easy balance, as you can imagine, when some folks want peace and quiet in their neighborhood and other folks want lots of action there. Because government has enormous power to advance or retard human harmony and justice, Christians take a lively interest in it. John Calvin even regarded government as a sign of God's love for us, a means of grace, because it adjusts life in society toward civil righteousness and promotes "general peace and tranquility."[6] In an unguarded moment Calvin went so far as to declare that "civil authority is a calling, not only holy and lawful before God, but also the most sacred and by far the most honorable of all callings in the whole life of mortal men."[7] Following Calvin, Reformed Christians have often thought that a government job was an especially strategic post within the kingdom of God, and that cynicism or apathy about government therefore amounts to a kind of apostasy, a loss of faith in God's grace. A citizen of the kingdom takes part in government — at minimum by voting intelligently, praying for leaders faithfully, and paying taxes willingly (I was going to write "cheerfully," but I knew you wouldn't buy that).

Besides government, God uses other institutions and groups to do some of the business of the kingdom, and Christians play their role in all of them. For instance, God uses industries to generate goods and services, hospitals to care for the hurt and sick, schools to educate intellectual seekers, recreational clubs to remind us of the need for a Seventh Day to filter through all the rest of our days. God uses Habitat for Humanity and, along the streets of the central part of Grand Rapids, the Inner City Christian Federation to provide high-

6. Calvin, *Institutes,* 2:1487 (4.20.2).
7. Calvin, *Institutes,* 2:1490 (4.20.4).

quality, affordable housing for people who might otherwise never know what it's like to live in a castle. When we open our eyes, we'll find faithful Christians seeking to extend God's sovereignty in every country, in every precinct of life, including such tough precincts as advertising, journalism, university education, and the military.

Explicitly Christian groups and institutions will come right out and say that their goal is to serve the kingdom of God. In fact, the group will likely write this goal into their institutional literature, as in the case of Calvin College, whose mission statement says that the college "seeks to engage in vigorous liberal arts education that promotes lives of Christian service." This statement is not just wishful thinking or good public relations. It's a public witness and solemn vow. The generations of faithful men and women whose prayers, money, intelligence, and hope have combined in this college have wanted one thing: they have wanted their college to "strive first for the kingdom of God" in the field of higher education.

But God needn't employ only Christian organizations to push forward the cause of his kingdom. God can use all kinds of groups

> "The priest anoints you on the forehead and puts on you the sign [of the cross], in order that the enemy may turn away his eyes. . . . Henceforth from that day there is strife and counterstrife with him, and on this account the priest leads you into the spiritual arena as athletes of Christ by virtue of this anointing."
>
> John Chrysostom[8]

8. St. John Chrysostom, *Baptismal Instructions,* trans. and ann. by Paul W. Harkins (Westminster, MD: The Newman Press, 1963), 52.

and persons to further his purposes, including groups and persons that are uninterested in God or even opposed to God. This is striking. After all, as theologians from Augustine to Calvin to Kuyper have written, God is at war with what is anti-God. The kingdom of God and the kingdom of this world are sworn foes, one centering in the glory of God and the triumph of grace, and the other centering in the glory of the creature and the triumph of his autonomy. In this connection, Augustine referred to "two cities formed by two loves," and Kuyper to the "antithesis" between belief and unbelief. According to their thinking, ever since the fall, Jerusalem and Athens, Christ and Satan, the church and the world have been engaged in a lengthy and uneven clash whose outcome has already been determined by the death and resurrection of Christ. But the clash still shows up everywhere, and not the least in education, where opposing philosophies really do grapple with each other for the minds of students.

On the one hand, then, we have the clashing of the kingdoms. On the other hand, as we saw in Chapter 3, we have the surprising fact that, owing to the common grace of God, the world is often better than we expect. Thus, when it comes to caring for the earth, for example, non-Christians often lead the way, showing more enthusiasm for good earthkeeping than conservative Christians who claim that "the earth is the Lord's," but who don't act that way.[9] It's true, of course, that some non-Christians want to care for the earth only because they tend toward materialist pantheism. Christians and Jews say, "the earth is the Lord's." Materialist pantheists say, "the earth is the Lord." But, ever the master of irony, God uses even the idolatrous philosophy of people who oppose him to get excellent earthkeeping out of them.

A prime citizen of the kingdom of God yearns for shalom, but non-Christians often yearn for at least a part of it too. Many non-Christians, even when they can't see Jesus Christ in their picture of "universal flourishing, wholeness, and delight" (the definition of sha-

9. Scott Hoezee, *Remember Creation: God's World of Wonder and Delight* (Grand Rapids: Eerdmans, 1998), 91-94.

lom back in Chapter 1), still want freedom and justice. They still desire truth and beauty. Indeed, as I just suggested with respect to the environment, some non-Christians long so passionately for these realities, and work so tirelessly for them, that they put Christians to shame. A person does not have to believe in Christ in order, unconsciously, to do a part of Christ's work in the world. "All truth is God's truth," as the philosopher Arthur Holmes has said, following the teaching of Augustine, and the same may be said of justice and beauty. The same may be said of healthy hope and of common grace and of every other good thing. God is the *summum bonum,* not only because he is by nature incorruptibly good, but also because he is the overflowing *source* of good. As we noted earlier, even the opponents of God need the gifts of God. They need these gifts just to lead a tolerable life. In fact, they need the gifts of God — energy, intelligence, creativity — even to oppose God. The Holy Spirit of God blows where it wills among people and nations, and often the Spirit blows outside the congregations of the faithful.

Christians follow their main vocation by playing a lively part in institutions and endeavors that, consciously or not, seek the interests

> I say móre: the just man justices;
> Keeps gráce: thát keeps all goings graces;
> Acts in God's eye what in God's eye he is —
> Chríst — for Christ plays in ten thousand places,
> Lovely in limbs, and lovely in eyes not his . . .
>
> Gerard Manley Hopkins[10]

10. Gerard Manley Hopkins, "As Kingfishers Catch Fire," in *Poems and Prose of Gerard Manley Hopkins,* selected and with an intro. and notes by W. H. Gardner (New York: Penguin Books, 1953, reprint 1985).

of the kingdom. Of these the church is first, but others — including governments, businesses, professions, and non-profit service organizations — are crucial as well. So are families. If they work right, families become a microcosm of the kingdom of God, incubating us in faith, hope, and love, schooling us in patience, supplying us with memories good enough to take out of storage on a lonely night. Families can give us our first lessons in meshing our kingdoms with others. They can fill us with delight, especially when they contain sunny, unspoiled toddlers.

> "Still, when we ask ourselves which persons in our lives mean the most to us, we often find that it is those who, instead of giving much advice, solutions, or cures, have chosen rather to share our pain and touch our wounds with a gentle and tender hand. The friend who can be silent with us in a moment of despair or confusion, who can stay with us in an hour of grief and bereavement, who can tolerate not-knowing, not-curing, not-healing and face with us the reality of our powerlessness, that is the friend who cares."
>
> Henri Nouwen[11]

To follow their main vocation of serving the kingdom of God, Christians pursue a wonderful array of sub-vocations. They sing, pray, and hand each other the body and blood of Christ. They rejoice with

11. Henri Nouwen, from *Out of Solitude: Three Meditations on the Christian Life* (Notre Dame, IN: Ave Maria, 1974), in *Seeds of Hope: A Henri Nouwen Reader,* ed. Robert Durback (New York: Bantam Books, 1989), 129.

those who rejoice and weep with those who weep. They fight against evil, but also fly kites and bake bread. As part of their vocation they absorb good books and good music. They work, but also rest from work in order to make a space in which to long for God. Some of them join volunteer groups that turn rails to trails, or that assist flood victims, or that paint somebody's house during *Streetfest*. In an emergency, an adult Christian might spend herself for a friend who is dying — sitting with her, praying with her, encouraging her, seeing to some of her needs. This isn't a job that appears on any government list of occupations, but it is a calling of God, and it is surely a contribution to the kingdom of God.

Speaking of occupations, let's notice now that what we call "getting a job" or "going to work" is only one way of participating in the various interests of the kingdom. Volunteering to teach Sunday school is another. So is stepping into a voting booth and making conscientious choices there. So is deciding whether to marry or to remain single, and, if married, whether to conceive or adopt children, or do both. These are all *vocational* decisions for a citizen of the kingdom, and some of them are large. But a Christian looks at even the smaller decisions (who deserves my support for the office of county drain commissioner?) with faith and good humor, aware that in the plan of God, the mustard seed of one of our decisions may combine with the mustard seeds of others' decisions to bring good growth for the kingdom.

Here we must avoid a common temptation to think of our vocation as no more than our job or career and to think of college as mere job training. It's easy to think that college is preparatory school for becoming, say, a dentist, or a city planner, or an elementary school teacher. According to this way of thinking, professors, college staff members, and parents or others who help with tuition — all these people are there mainly to help us get a good job.

Not so. Of course, professors and others will be pleased if you get a good job. Good work is worth doing, and the world needs plenty of people who do it well. Moreover, a superb education at Calvin College will indeed make you employable in respectable places. But thinking of college as no more than job training is a narrow-minded impoverishment of the kingdom of God. That's like thinking that a flight attendant needs to be an alert person mainly to remember people's drink orders. Of course, alertness does come in handy when it comes time to take and fill an order. But that's not the only, and not even the central, reason why a flight attendant ought to be alert.

"God's other name is 'Surprise.'"

Chaplain Dale Cooper

So let's think again about your college education. Your degree will certainly make you more employable, but, so far as the kingdom is concerned, that's only one dimension of the value of your education. The full value of your education is that it will help you find and prepare for your vocation — which, as we've just seen, is much bigger than any particular occupation. In fact, you might retire from a very different occupation than the one in which you started, and you might have tried several others in the interim. In any event, your college education is meant to prepare you for prime citizenship in the kingdom of God. For four years or so, such preparation is itself a big part of your vocation. Your calling is to prepare for further calling, and to do so in a Christian college community that cares as much about the kind of person you are becoming as what kind of job you will eventually get, and as much about *how* you will do your job as about *which* job you do.

Still, career choices do matter, and college is a natural place to think about them. God does endow us with particular gifts and interests that better equip us for kingdom service in some fields than in others. Not all of us have what it takes to be ballet dancers, for example. We're not tough enough.

117

> *"The place God calls you to is the place where your deep gladness and the world's deep hunger meet."*
>
> Frederick Buechner[12]

Most North American college students consider various career paths while they are still in school, and many invest a good deal of energy in finding a path that seems right for them. A Christian does too. But a Christian may approach such a decision in faith and without the panicky feeling that "I've *got* to get this degree to be competitive." A Christian has more poise. Like everybody else, she'll assess her gifts and interests. She'll think of what kind of work she could do naturally, in sync with her temperament and approaches to life. She'll study the job market. Like others, she will probably notice how lucrative and prestigious her potential career might be, especially if she thinks of entering a demanding profession. But if she's "striving first for the kingdom" she will deliberately bracket considerations of big money and prestige in favor of more important issues.

To "strive first for the kingdom" in choosing a career, a Christian will ask himself particular questions. Where in the kingdom does God want me to work? Where are the needs great? Where are the workers few?

> *"When Christ calls a man, he bids him come and die."*
>
> Dietrich Bonhoeffer[13]

Where are the temptations manageable? With whom would I work? How honest is the work I'm thinking of doing? How necessary and how healthy are the goods or services I would help provide? How smoothly could I combine my proposed career with being a spouse, if

---

12. Frederick Buechner, *Wishful Thinking: A Seeker's ABC,* rev. and expanded (San Francisco: HarperSanFrancisco, 1993), 119.

13. Dietrich Bonhoeffer, *The Cost of Discipleship* (New York: Simon & Schuster, 1995), 89. I owe the juxtaposition of these two sidebars to L. Gregory Jones.

that's also my calling, or a parent, or a faithful child of aging parents? How close would I be to a church in which I could give and take nourishment? Is my proposed career inside a system so corrupt that, even with the best intentions, I would end up absorbing a lot more evil than I conquer?

Placing emphasis where Jesus placed it, a prime citizen will add another question: What would my career do for "the least of these"?

What all of these questions express is an interest in serving the common good. God has ordered human society in such a way that we all depend on each other. Before we give thanks for our daily bread, somebody has to have baked it. In fact, before a slice of honey oatmeal appears on our plate, a number of farmers, millers, bakers, distributors, drivers, grocers, and others have had to work together in order to supply our need. This is a commercial arrangement, but not *only* a commercial arrangement. As Calvin professor Lee Hardy has written, it's also a social arrangement that expresses and reinforces our dependence on each other. God *intends* "that human beings should live in a society bound together by common needs and mutual service."[14] In fact, our dependence on each other is so profound, and so much a part of the meshing of our kingdoms inside God's kingdom, that when Jesus wanted to illustrate how to receive the kingdom of God he pointed to a baby. "Whoever does not receive the kingdom of God as a little child will never enter it," he said (Luke 18:17). Jesus almost surely meant that before we ever have anything to give, before we're ever ready to build a barn or dig a well, we have to learn how to become good *receivers*. Infants don't do much. They just lie around all day. But they are perfectly wonderful receivers, and therefore they are our teachers when it comes to one of the relationships — dependence — that ties us to each other and to God.

---

14. Lee Hardy, *The Fabric of This World: Inquiries into Calling, Career Choice, and the Human Design of Work* (Grand Rapids: Eerdmans, 1990), 60.

God Loveth Adverbs

At the end of the last chapter we saw that God's program of redemption is all-encompassing. Wherever life has been corrupted, it needs to be reformed. Accordingly, a prime citizen of the kingdom will typically be a reform-minded citizen, looking for ways to address some of the deformities in human life and culture. As you know, reform happens in many ways. It may occur when a nation gets shamed into seeing its injustice (think of civil rights legislation) or its carelessness (think of new building codes that require wheelchair accessibility). It may occur when the conscientious efforts of good people in business, medicine, law, labor, education, and elsewhere gain sufficient momentum so as to make a positive difference in those fields.

Some of these reforms are led by Christian people who genuinely hope for the kingdom of God. Some are led by non-Christian people moved by a simple desire for truth or justice. Many are led by people with mixed motives. But every genuine advance toward shalom is led by the Holy Spirit, who promiscuously chooses instruments of God's peace. In any case, Christian people seek the gift of discernment to know when and how to join existing movements toward shalom and when and how to start new ones.

But here a word of caution is in order. It's one thing to talk about reform, and another to do it. Reformed Christians have been good at talking, and writing, and talking some more. And some have been pretty good at doing, too. But it's possible for reform-minded people to overestimate their rhetoric and underestimate the job. Some social realities are extremely resistant to reform. Great money, power, or pleasure supports them. Great acceptance surrounds them. Long traditions sustain them. Some of these realities therefore seem irredeemable, or nearly so. Racism, for example, is an evil of great staying power. People may reform their speech and practice where racial relations are concerned, but the reforms don't always stick, and sometimes they don't make it all the way through to people's hearts. Or people reform for a while and then backslide. Moreover, racism can work its way from people's hearts into the structure of institutions, where it is sometimes hard to get at. Or, besides racism, take an old problem of which you may have recent memories: What would have to happen for high school students to quit forming into cliques that marginalize or even terrorize their weak or unpopular classmates?

> *"One of the most blasphemous consequences of injustice, especially racist injustice, is that it can make a child of God doubt that he or she is a child of God."*
>
> Desmond Mpilo Tutu[15]

John Calvin believed that an unredeemed life keeps oscillating back and forth between pride ("I've made it!") and despair ("I'll never make it"). In his view, redemption gives people security, or (one of Calvin's favorite words) *repose*. His idea was that those who lean into God's grace and let it hold them up can then drop some of their performance anxiety.

Perhaps the same pattern holds for Christians' approach to reforming culture. On the one hand, we need to avoid triumphalism, the prideful view that we Christians will fully succeed in transforming all or much of culture. No doubt triumphalists underestimate some of the difficulties. They may underestimate cultural ironies too. After all, the history of the world is full of revolutions that Christians hailed as part of the coming of God's kingdom, only to discover that the revolutions ended up generating as much tyranny as they displaced.

On the other hand, we also need to avoid the despairing tendency

15. Desmond Mpilo Tutu, *No Future without Forgiveness* (New York: Doubleday, 1999), 197.

to write the world off, to abandon it as a lost cause, and to remove ourselves to an island of like-minded Christians. The world, after all, belongs to God and is in the process of being redeemed by God. "God so loved the world that he gave his only Son . . . in order that the world might be saved through him" (John 3:16-17). Indeed, God's plan is to gather up *all things* in Christ. How bizarre it would be for Christians to turn their backs on this plan. How ungrateful it would be to receive the bread of life and then refuse to share it with others.

As a matter of fact, Christians have been put in a solid position where the reform of culture is concerned: we have been invited to live beyond triumphalism and despair, spending ourselves for a cause that we firmly believe will win in the end. So, on the one hand, we don't need to take responsibility for trying to fix everything. The earth is the Lord's, and he will save it. On the other hand, we may take responsibility for contributing what we uniquely *have* to contribute to the kingdom, joining with many others from across the world who are striving to be faithful, to add the work of their hands and minds to the eventual triumph of God.

Meanwhile, none of us is stuck with trying to promote the kingdom of God with an occupation we can't stand. At one time people were born into their occupations, so that the son of a farmer, for example, was simply expected to take over the family farm. If he wanted to do something else with his life he was thought to be peculiar or, worse, traitorous. But, as Nicholas Wolterstorff has written, Reformed Christians of the sixteenth and seventeenth centuries rejected the old idea that each of us is born to be just one thing — a butcher, a baker, a candlestick maker. Instead, each of us must find an occupation so intrinsically valuable and so naturally suited to us that, through it, we may add to the treasure of the kingdom. In fact, adds Wolterstorff, we must not only find an occupation to bring to the kingdom; we must also *shape* it to suit this purpose.[16]

The point is that occupations are often valuable to the kingdom, but only if we reform them. So in today's world, perhaps a Christian

16. Wolterstorff, *Justice and Peace,* 17.

122

would shape the occupation of quality-control supervisor by encouraging whistle-blowers instead of retaliating against them. Perhaps a Christian would shape the occupation of computer repair technician by doing top-notch diagnoses in order to save customers the expense of unnecessary repairs. Perhaps a Christian would shape the occupation of CEO of a major airline by telling its customers the truth about flight cancellations and delays. In any case, occupational reforms serve the kingdom of God as surely as a Billy Graham Crusade does.

Only a few of us will launch great reform movements, and even fewer of us will do it deliberately. But all of us may offer our gifts and energies to the cause of God's program in the world. When we make this offering by means of an ordinary occupation, we will sometimes feel as if our *lives* are very ordinary. No matter. An ordinary occupation done conscientiously builds the kingdom of God. Jesus built the kingdom as a carpenter before he built it as a rabbi. And he taught us in the parable of the talents that the question for disciples is not *which* callings they have but how faithfully they pursue them. In remarking on this theme, the Puritan Joseph Hall wrote:

> The homeliest service that we doe in an honest calling, though it be but to plow, or digge, if done in obedience, and conscience of God's Commandement, is crowned with an ample reward; whereas the best workes for their kinde (preaching, praying, offering Evangelicall sacrifices) if without respect of God's injunction and glory, are loaded with curses. God loveth adverbs; and cares not how good, but how well.[17]

Vocation and Education

A college education can help a Christian follow his vocation, including its occupational component. Secular higher education is also one

---

17. Quoted in Charles H. George and Katherine George, *The Protestant Mind of the English Reformation* (Princeton: Princeton University, 1961), 139n.

of the tools God can use for this purpose, but it's often a blunt one. Mainstream education isn't set up to help students form a Christian philosophy of life and vocation, including a philosophy of good and evil derived from sustained reflection on the drama of creation, fall, and redemption. In fact, it's common in postmodern secular education to reject all "meta-narratives" of the kind that the biblical story represents — that is, stories that transcend their own cultural setting and purport to be universally true. (What could be more presumptuous, postmodernists think, than to suppose that the biblical account of creation, fall, and redemption explains *human* life, and not just the lives of Bible believers!) In secular academia, religious approaches to learning are generally unwelcome — sometimes dismissed, but more often simply ignored. Thus it would be unusual in an Ivy League classroom to find a discussion of spiral and elliptical galaxies that referred not only to their beauty and immensity but also to the even greater beauty and immensity of their Creator. It would be rare to find a discussion of economic relations that focused on the spiritual significance of poverty or of consumerism.[18] It would be uncommon in a discussion of racism to find it rejected because it fails to honor the image of God in other human beings. The biblical account of God's creation of all human beings in his image is, after all, another of those forbidden meta-narratives.

Predictably enough, secular education tends to promote a secular view of the world and of human life, routinely giving students the impression that theistic accounts of reality have become passé, that they aren't important enough to be considered, that educated people don't think about them much. Moreover, secular education is plagued by various falsehoods and confusions that have become fashionable in postmodernity — that God is dead, or, alternatively, that God interferes with human autonomy and ought to stop; that there isn't any

---

18. In "Religion-free Texts: Getting an Illiberal Education," *Christian Century,* July 14-21, 1999, 711-15, Warren A. Nord demonstrates that public high school textbooks "systematically exclude religious voices." Many of his observations apply to secular education more generally, including secular higher education.

such thing as truth; that it is wicked to make moral judgments (think that one over); that our main aim as human beings is self-expression or even self-deification; that right and wrong are whatever anybody thinks they are; that power trumps all else; and so on.[19]

Christian students on secular campuses may expect to stand against these ideas without caving in to them and without hardening into pious anti-intellectuals. If so, they expect a lot. And if they expect to develop a mature Christian philosophy of life without the help of their professors — in fact, with the *hindrance* of some of their professors — they expect even more. I acknowledge that an unusual Christian student might rise to the challenge. He might telephone people for help, read books outside of class, join InterVarsity Christian Fellowship, consult with the campus chaplain in the hope that she could offer him a small co-curriculum of Christian Perspectives on Learning. He might join an organization specifically designed to think Christianly about major campus topics, such as the superb Veritas Forum at Harvard University. He might even have the courage to try out his faith in class. His idea would be that you can dare to be a Daniel only if you spend time in the lions' den, and his idea is definitely worth considering. In fact, every Christian community includes some Daniels who made it through the academic dens of confusion and conformity with their kingdom vocation intact and sometimes even purified by the fires of adversity.

But I fear that for most Christian students mainstream higher education simply won't be adequate to help them understand the kingdom of God and their own vocation within it. Such students will be busy with a hundred other things and won't take the time or spend the effort to sort out the good and evil in what they encounter on campus and to construct a thoughtful Christian philosophy of life on their own. They will find it easier to go with the flow, sometimes aware of dissonances between their faith and their learning and between their faith and their campus life, sometimes unaware that they

---

19. Alvin Plantinga, *Warranted Christian Belief* (New York: Oxford University, 2000), 423.

are absorbing views of the world and of life that flatly contradict the gospel. Content with personal prayer, personal witnessing, and small-group Bible study as ways of being Christian on campus, a number of these students will live with a wall between their sacred faith and their secular learning.

The founders and leaders of Calvin College have tried to imagine "a more excellent way." They have designed a program of higher education that refuses to separate the sacred from the secular, believing with Abraham Kuyper that of every square inch of human existence Jesus Christ proclaims, "This is Mine." A Calvin education therefore centers where the Christian life itself must center, namely on Christ the Lord of all. As the college said in 1997 when it adopted a Statement of Purpose for the new core curriculum:

> Christians seek to live their whole lives in continuity with Christ, taking on his mind and affections, acting as his body in the world, sharing his sufferings and his victories in the project of overcoming misery and rebuilding God's good creation. Christians gladly join this project out of gratitude to Christ, out of obedience to Christ, and out of an enkindled desire to work within the Kingdom of Christ. As faithful workers within this Kingdom, Christians struggle to align themselves with the redemptive purposes of God in this world.[20]

Education at a Christian college such as Calvin is meant to demonstrate this "continuity with Christ" and therefore to line up "with the redemptive purposes of God in the world." Or put it like this: your Calvin education is designed to help you love the Lord our God with all your *mind,* and then to love your neighbor as yourself with a life of educated service. In this way, your Christian higher education may serve both as your present vocation and as your preparation for a life-long vocation as a prime citizen of the kingdom.

20. Preface to "An Engagement with God's World: A Statement of Purpose for the Core Curriculum," in Appendix III, 178-79.

How so? How does Christian higher education work? What's the process?

Day to day, the process is one of gaining the knowledge, skills, and virtues you will need to make your contribution to the kingdom of God. Faculty, staff, and other students will help you acquire these things.

But a word of caution: just as it would be a huge mistake simply to go with the flow on a secular campus, so it's a huge mistake to suppose you can get truly educated by floating downstream in a Christian college. An education is something you have to achieve; it's almost something you have to win. I mean that a seasoned Christian approach to the world and human life requires a real struggle with alternative approaches. A maturing Christian has to think about them,

> *"And the thought came to me, sudden and shocking, that the broken and contrite heart is something far more terrible than penitence."*
>
> Alan Paton[21]

wonder about them, try to see what's attractive and partly true in them. If you have come to Calvin College so you won't have to wrestle with Nietzsche or worry about evolution, you've come to the wrong school. You can't "rise with Christ" unless you've died with him first, and that means enduring some dark nights of the soul.

The disciples could not "watch with me even one hour," as Jesus lamented, and it has always been a temptation for Christian students (and their parents) to want a safe college where there are no intellectual or existential Gethsemanes. But this is an illusion. It may even be a kind of cowardice. The truth is that a student who is trying — under

21. Alan Paton, *Too Late the Phalarope* (New York: Simon & Schuster, 1995), 275.

sure-handed supervision — to learn a mature Christian approach to the world will have to take some pain, including the pain of doubt or of indecision. In fact, if you are a doubter, the Bible is your book. It's full of the doubts and laments of believers whose faith emerges only from a crucible of some kind. Jesus' own lament from the cross, "My God, my God, why have you forsaken me?" (Mark 15:34) has become one of the most famous things he said, a small death during his big death.

Followers of Jesus struggle not only with their work but also with their prayers, with their meditations, with attempting to open spaces at the depths where the Spirit of God may descend and dwell. The spiritual disciplines (prayer, study, meditation, confession) look as if they would be a pain; and they are. But they are also a joy. They look as if they would bind us. They do, but they bind our own internal constraints — the desires that lead us around if we do not bind them. So the disciplines actually open a door to freedom. The discipline of study can feel like a burden. It is a burden, but the Christian person yokes up with Jesus Christ to haul the burden, and the joy and freedom of fellowship with Christ make the burden light. In short, the disciplines help make us prime citizens of the kingdom because they help to make us strong and deep.

> *"Superficiality is the curse of our age. The doctrine of instant satisfaction is a primary spiritual problem.*
> *The desperate need today is not for a greater number of intelligent people, or gifted people, but for deep people."*
>
> Richard J. Foster[22]

22. Richard J. Foster, *Celebration of Discipline: The Path to Spiritual Growth* (San Francisco: Harper & Row, 1978), 1.

As a person with responsible dominion in the world, you will need to take responsibility for your own education, *seeing to it* that you gain the knowledge, hone the skills, and develop the virtues you'll need now and later in order to play your role in the drama of the kingdom. The college's Statement of Purpose for the core curriculum includes a full treatment of these components, and you can find it attached below as part of Appendix III. Meanwhile, here's a sampling, largely from that document, of the knowledge, skills, and virtues the college thinks you'll need in order to find and follow your vocation.

Knowledge

We want a body of knowledge in order to love God intellectually, as well as every other way, and also in order to identify and address human needs, including our own. For these purposes we need knowledge of the triune God; of creation, fall, and redemption; of the tenets and practices of the Christian religion — all of this knowledge leading naturally to the development of a "Christian world-and-life view." With such a view, and with increasing knowledge of the natural world, human society, history, the arts, and our own identities and callings, a Christian student will be able at some point to take an educated position on such issues and questions as these:

- how the world's other major religions might simultaneously express serious confusions and also the *sensus divinitatis* with which God has endowed the whole human race;
- whether history is the sad tale of decline from an old golden age, or the heartening story of progress toward a new one, or (depending on how these ages are understood) both, or neither;
- how quantitative structures represent not only "the alphabet in which God wrote the universe" but also a primary alphabet of social research methods and of public policy;
- why land shapes human culture, and why human culture shapes

land, and what these shapings might have to do with responsible
dominion;

- whether economic growth in the capitalist economy of a developing nation is likely to be cruel or kind or both;
- what it means to belong to a community in covenant with God;
- why a work of art might ennoble life in one way and degrade it in
another;
- how to explain the rise of mall-speak among North American
middle school students ("He goes *'Yes!'* and I'm, like, 'Whoa!') and
how to assess its significance.

Skills

Beyond a body of knowledge, a student also needs to acquire, or
sharpen, an array of skills. These enable a student to prevail not only
in class and on campus but also in a host of vocational settings
throughout life. Skills are "how to" disciplines that, like all disciplines, require a certain amount of sweat and repetition, and then
yield some wonderful freedoms. (Think, for example, of a jazz musi-
cian improvising on a rhythmic or melodic theme and of the combination of discipline and freedom that's displayed in the improvisa-
tion.)

An educated student will possess some combination of such skills
as these. She'll know how to:

- construct and test an argument for a thesis;
- argue without quarreling;
- read and correlate tables of statistics and judge their relevance to
a proposed business plan;
- use a Versaport Slider;
- spot an idol;
- write a clear sentence and sometimes a lively one;
- identify and interpret tropes;
- understand and speak a second language;

> *"My brother, Cecil Edward Chesterton, was born when I was about five years old; and, after a brief pause, began to argue. He continued to argue to the end. . . . I am glad to think that through all those years we never stopped arguing; and we never once quarrelled. Perhaps the principal objection to a quarrel is that it interrupts an argument."*
>
> G. K. Chesterton[23]

- form and follow a sound research plan;
- square up for a shot;
- play an arpeggio in tune;
- speak a strengthening word to a discouraged prof without angling for a better grade.

A little reflection tells us that Christians want such skills not to impress the less skillful and not simply to become more employable. Christians hope to increase the net amount of shalom in the world. Thus, a clearly written sentence not only conveys a thought or raises a question; it also saves readers from unnecessary confusion. A well-executed piece of team defense not only leads toward victory; it also delights viewers who understand its intelligence. Learning a second language not only equips a person to pursue business or art in new venues; it also respects strangers and opens the way for hospitality to them.[24] Along these lines, knowledge and skills often enable a person to express

23. G. K. Chesterton, *Autobiography* (London: Hutchinson, 1937), 196.

24. For this last possibility see *The Gift of the Stranger: Faith, Hospitality, and Foreign Language Learning* (Grand Rapids: Eerdmans, 2000) by Calvin College professors Barbara M. Carvill and David I. Smith.

> *"The approach to style is by way of plainness, simplicity, orderliness, sincerity. . . . Muddiness is not merely a disturber of prose, it is also a destroyer of life, of hope."*
>
> E. B. White[25]

not only the critical discernment of a prophet but also the committed heart of a servant.

Virtues

Classical education has always encouraged students to acquire more than knowledge and skills; it has also encouraged them to develop the virtues that will incline them to use these things for the benefit of others. Christians believe that such virtues derive from the Holy Spirit and that this is so no matter who has them. But, as we saw in Chapter 4, Christians have special reason for cultivating honesty, compassion, and other good traits. These virtues suit Christians. They're part of dying and rising with Christ and therefore part of the family uniform for the people of God. It's extremely *fitting* for those who have received grace at so great a cost to offer it to others, and by doing so to build up not only the church, but also the kingdom of God.

As the college's Statement of Purpose for the Core Curriculum says:

Virtues are settled dispositions to feel and act in certain ways. A compassionate person is inclined, as if by nature, to be moved by human suffering. A person in possession of the vir-

25. E. B. White, "An Approach to Style," in William Strunk and E. B. White, *The Elements of Style* (New York: Macmillan, 1959), 57, 65.

tue of honesty has the disposition to tell the truth. Vices are also dispositions. A callous person, bearing within the breast a heart of stone, disregards the needs of others as a matter of habit. A person saddled with the vice of deceitfulness has the disposition to lie whenever lying seems convenient. A particular array of virtues and vices, taken together, makes up a person's character.[26]

Let's be clear about the nature of dispositions. A compassionate person is one who not only *doesn't* close his heart to human suffering; he *wouldn't* do so. An honest person not only *doesn't* lie or steal; she *wouldn't* do these things. If she ever did, she would feel out of sync, out of step with herself. A virtuous person needs rules the way a golfer needs "checkpoints" in squaring himself up for a good tee shot. He needs the checkpoints to learn a solid setup for a shot, but after many repetitions a person makes a practice of feeling and doing what's right. He "has a habit" where virtue is concerned, and so he naturally does what's right.

In a Christian college we learn and practice virtues in ways that fit into the dynamic process of teaching and learning, the process of preparation for the several dimensions of a life's calling. We learn such virtues as

- diligence, the inclination to dig in for the long haul, to "keep on keeping on" in the face of intellectual obstacles or other difficulties;
- patience, the readiness to absorb irritants without letting them paralyze us;
- charity, the inclination to give others — including authors we dislike — the benefit of the doubt, putting the best face on their words and motives;
- stewardship, the disposition to take good care not only of the world's resources but also of our own, so that we students, fac-

26. "An Engagement with God's World," in Appendix III, 226.

ulty, and staff spend time, money, energy, and intelligence on pursuits that really do answer God's calling, and not just our own whims.

Q. What is God's will for you
in the ninth commandment?
A. God's will is that I
never give false testimony against anyone,
twist no one's words,
not gossip or slander,
nor join in condemning anyone
without a hearing or without a just cause.

Heidelberg Catechism,
Question and Answer 112

"Character is destiny," said the ancient Greek thinker Heraclitus. How we feel and act in classrooms and labs, on stages and playing fields, with friends and strangers will lead us toward one future rather than another. The charitable person, for example, will discover friends among those that the uncharitable person simply dismisses. The truth-telling person will move good projects forward because she has traction on reality. The patient person will always be hard to defeat and will therefore often win through to first-class achievements.

In fact, when a well-educated person combines knowledge, skills, and virtues to pursue God's calling — whether or not he is conscious of it — the result may be remarkable. I could cite a number of examples, but consider just one that has to do with your vision.

Given the number of maladies that can afflict it — whether because of a retinal defect or because of the brain's misapprehending

> *"You don't always have to chop with the sword of truth. You can point with it, too."*
>
> Anne Lamott[27]

what the eye is perceiving — it's amazing that any one of us should have 20/20, Kodak-color vision without corrective lenses.

In the early 1980s, Dr. Helen Irlen was conducting research on adults who'd been diagnosed with dyslexia. The results of her research soon presented a pattern among some: those who preferred to read in dim light also said they preferred not to read black print on white paper. Instead they favored, say, black words on red paper or purple paper — some color that was less of a contrast to the black. When the contrast was great, they said, words on a page faded in or out, or leaped around, or became like islands in a delta with little white rivers flowing between them.[28]

While most of the people in her study said that they experienced this phenomenon only while they were reading, a few noted that they endured bizarre visual distortions all the time. They felt as if they lived in an animated "house of mirrors" where sidewalks buckled, buildings folded, and fire hydrants needed a leash. Using computer imaging, one young woman, Alex, was able to re-create her symptoms of "scotopic sensitivity" so that Dr. Irlen could better understand it. Eventually Dr. Irlen discovered that if Alex wore glasses tinted just the right shade of blue, Alex's animated world ceased its assault.

Today tinted lenses are used to correct the vision of thousands who suffer from dyslexia, scotopic sensitivity, or color blindness. In each case, a simple tinted lens "tricks" the brain into reinterpreting

27. Anne Lamott, *Bird by Bird* (New York: Doubleday, 1995), 156.
28. Paul R. Whiting, "How Difficult Can Reading Be?" *Parent & Citizen* 44, no. 4 (1993): 12-18.

what the eye says it sees. By combining knowledge, skill, and virtue, Dr. Irlen developed an imaginative address to three maladies, and thereby served the kingdom of God.

How good it is when human beings serve in such ways. How wonderful it is when they do it in conscious acknowledgment of the calling of God and in faith that, between this life and the next, between the partial coming of the kingdom and the full coming of the kingdom, nothing good will ever be lost.

Epilogue

■ ■ ■ ■ ■

*The earth is the LORD's and all that is in it,
the world, and those who live in it.*

Psalm 24:1

*God blessed Noah and his sons, and said to them, "Be fruit-
ful, and multiply, and fill the earth. . . . I establish my covenant with you, that . . . never again shall there be a flood to
destroy the earth."*

Genesis 9:1, 11

*"Then they will see 'the Son of Man coming in a cloud' with
power and great glory."*

Luke 21:27-28

*Then I saw a new heaven and a new earth . . . and I saw the
holy city, the new Jerusalem, coming down out of heaven
from God. . . . And I heard a loud voice from the throne saying, "See, the home of God is among mortals."*

Revelation 21:1-3a

I've been writing all along that education is for service in the kingdom of God — or for shalom in God's kingdom. Our education matters, and I now want to add that it matters not only for this world but also for the world to come. My reason for thinking so is that Scripture appears to teach not only that there shall be a new heaven and earth, but also that it shall be *this* earth, renewed. In Revelation 21 the city of God descends to us. We do not go to heaven; heaven comes to us. In a vision lovely enough to break a person's heart, John shows us what God showed him, that up ahead of us, after centuries of tribal feuds and racial arrogance, after centuries of xenophobic snapping at each other, after we human beings have silted history full with the debris of all our antagonisms — after all that, the city of God will descend to us, and God will dwell with us, and, once more, God will make all things new.

The Old Testament prophecies of shalom — of perfect justice, harmony, and delight among God, human beings, and all creation — apply neither to the present church (of which in any case they are not true) nor to a future existence in a distant, airy heaven. These prophecies apply to the future of a very solid, tangible, visible earth.[1] Or to the earth and a number of other planets. Fripp Island, S.C., will be a part of heaven. So will the Lake District in England, the Schwarzwald of southwest Germany, and the Great Barrier Reef off the eastern coast of Australia. Banff will be included and the islands of Indonesia. Kenya's game preserves will still draw visitors, and so will the mountains of northeast Korea. There is an outside chance for Grand Rapids, once 28th Street has been converted to a multi-lane bike path, lined on each side by seasonal flowers and copper beech trees.

In this vision, one can spot lines of continuity between the work of Christ in the present and in the future, between the small whispers and hints now and the final cosmic renewal and triumph of the Lamb. What we do now in the name of Christ — striving for healing, for justice, for intellectual light in darkness, striving simply to produce something helpful for sustaining the lives of other human be-

1. Anthony A. Hoekema, *The Bible and the Future* (Grand Rapids: Eerdmans, 1979), 281-87.

ings — shall be preserved across into the next life. All of it counts, all of it lasts, none of it is wasted or lost. All of it acts like salt that eventually seasons a whole slab of meat, or a seed that grows one day into a tree that looks nothing like the seed at all.

For there is both cultural continuity and transformation in the link between this world and the next. As we know, twisted culture now fills the earth. God's mandate to "multiply and fill the earth" has been answered too often by strip mines, oil slicks, and denuded rain forests; too often by dictatorships and ethnic cleansing; too often by computerized dope distribution schemes. Great scientists use their excellent minds to dream up weapons that find their way into the hands of terrorists. Television writers put a good face on godlessness. Ministers use their seminary training to preach gospels in which all the difficult bits about sin and grace have been purposely razored away. "Multiply and fill the earth," said God after the flood. And the earth is now full. The trouble is that it's full of our trash as well as God's treasure.

Remarkably, God wants the earth anyhow. God wants it back. Why? What's the point? The earth's trash is, after all, the product of our fallenness, of our disobedience. It's the product and encouragement of human arrogance. Why doesn't God flush it all away with another deluge?

Because God has promised to preserve the earth. As you recall, Genesis 9 records God's promise never again to destroy the earth with a flood. The point is that the earth is the Lord's. The point is that the earth *in all its fullness* is the Lord's. God means to reclaim the fullness that is his. But just as you and I have to be converted, so does all of culture. Swords will have to be turned back into pruning shears, switchblades into paring knives, and spears into garden hoes. High-powered dope-running speedboats — cigarette boats — will have to be reclaimed for teaching poor children to water-ski. In the new heaven and earth, intercontinental ballistic missile silos will be transformed into training tanks for scuba divers.[2]

2. Richard J. Mouw, *When the Kings Come Marching In: Isaiah and the New Jerusalem* (Grand Rapids: Eerdmans, 1983), 16-20.

In a thousand ways, God will gather what's scattered, rebuild what's broken, restore what has been emptied out by centuries of waste and fraud. In a thousand ways, God will put right what's wrong with his glorious creation. In fact, the Bible hints that the new heaven and earth may *surpass* the original creation: marriage, for instance, will no longer be necessary for human fellowship at its deepest level (Mark 12:25).

The earth is the Lord's, in all its fullness. We have corrupted the earth through folly and sin, but God means to restore all things in the harmony, justice, and delight of shalom. This is a sign to us: On the third day Jesus Christ rose again from the dead, the pledge that one day all things shall be renewed. And God has called people like us to become agents for the restoration project that is already in process. These agents need to be educated. More than we could ever think or say, Christian education is for this project. Christian education is the training of special agents of the kingdom of God and the consummation of creation. That's why you are at Calvin College. That's why all of us — students, faculty, staff, administrators — spend our time, spend our money, spend ourselves in Christian higher education.

Meanwhile, don't imagine that while you're in college you're in some kind of holding tank awaiting the great day when you'll emerge into the "real world." People will speak of college life to you in this way, saying things like, "Just wait till you get to the *real* world." Often what they mean is "just wait till you get out here where balancing work and leisure is nearly impossible and keeping up with debts is a real headache." If that's the "real world," then you're definitely in the thick of it as a student.

But jobs, bills, and stress aren't necessarily the "real world" either, or at least not anything like the whole of it. To think in that way is to think small. No matter what our primary occupation, we can't let it become a preoccupation, though that's a usual temptation. Even now, when we get really focused on cramming for tests and cranking out papers, it's easy to let the rest of reality fade into the background. Soon the world is no bigger than our dorm room, a classroom, and the sidewalks in between. And that's not the real world at all.

Someone who lives in the "real world" lives with an awareness of the *whole* world, because the *whole* world is part of the kingdom of God. On any given day he may walk no more than a mile, but his imagination will trot the globe.

While you're at Calvin, I hope you'll find it perfectly natural to let your mind wander in this way, not aimlessly, but purposefully. One of the goals of education, after all, is to shrink our provincialism and to enlarge our horizons.

One obvious way to become acquainted with the world is to immerse yourself in another culture for a time. Did you know that during any given school year there are more than fifty opportunities to study abroad, whether for interim or a semester? Maybe you'll travel to the Galapagos Islands to study tropical flora and fauna and to see how conservationists are preserving the delicate ecosystem there. Or maybe one fall you'll spend a semester in Hungary, exploring the history, culture, and politics of a Central European nation that's struggling for identity in the post–Cold War era. Or maybe you'll live in Honduras for a semester, gaining firsthand experience of third-world poverty and the development efforts to relieve it. Having studied abroad, students often report that their experience has expanded and complicated their understanding of the kingdom of God in ways they could never have guessed. Often they report that their hope for the new heaven and earth has picked up speed.

Then again, maybe you're already immersing yourself in another culture simply by coming to Calvin. Maybe you've flown through the airspace of fifteen different countries on three different continents and had your passport checked a half-dozen times before you even arrived in the United States. If you are an international student, you bring the world to us in a way that the news and *National Geographic* never could. Sometimes we'll be shy about asking you questions, afraid of exposing our ignorance. Still, while you're exploring American culture, we hope you'll give us more than a glimpse of your own country's culture, broadening our horizons even as you broaden your own.

International travel is wonderful, but it's not the only — nor even the most expedient — way to stir our imaginations and increase our knowledge of the world. That's why many educated people pick up a credible newspaper every day, either on-line or off the stand. Maybe the best we can do in a busy week is scan the headlines. Even so, we'll spot some part of the drama of the kingdom that is destined to come one day in all its fullness.

The same opportunities present themselves in much of the curriculum and co-curriculum at Calvin, where we can meet various cultures right on campus or in the neighborhoods of Grand Rapids. Student organizations expand our imaginations too, whether they grapple with contemporary issues, produce entertainment, or explore a profession. Campus worship expresses the drama of the kingdom every day, as we join the voices of Christians from around the world and throughout all of history to extol our Creator, to intercede for his people, and to anticipate future glory. Every campus publication — *Chimes, Dialogue, Spark, The Undercurrent* — is distributed (free) at the newsstand on the corner. The kiosk opposite publicizes concerts, plays, lectures, and art gallery exhibits.

In each of these places and events, something of creation, fall, and redemption comes to us. In each of these venues we encounter the real world through some medium. The same benefit comes to those who invest energy in Service-Learning. For you, it began with StreetFest, nearly the day you arrived on campus. The experience was brief. Still, I hope you've caught a glimpse of what a teachable experience a few hours of service can be. As children we're taught that it's rude to expect something in return for something we've given. Could it be that Service-Learning is a delightful exception? It seems so, since we take up our role as a servant fully expecting to learn something from those we serve.

None of these venues is an escape from the real world; they are all doorways into it. When we pass through, we hear the world's celebrations and laments. If we listen with empathy, we discover what it means to hope the world's hopes — or maybe hope against them — for the sake of the kingdom of God.

According to Scripture, the person who wants the restoration of the earth wants the kingdom of God whether she knows it or not.

And the coming of the kingdom depends on the coming of the King, the one who will return "with power and great glory" (Luke 21:27). However we are to understand this apocalyptic event, whatever form it takes, the second coming of Jesus Christ means to a Christian that God's righteousness will at last fill the earth, and that the real world in all its trouble and turmoil will be transformed by God's shalom.

People with crummy lives want it to happen now. Passionate Christians *want* the return of the Lord. And, let me add, so do compassionate ones. When our own life is sweet, we can look across the world to lives that aren't sweet. We can raise our heads and our hopes for those lives. We can weep with those who weep and hope with those who hope. We can look across the world, and across the room, and across the hall. Could justice really come to the earth? Could husbands quit beating up their wives, and could wives quit blaming themselves? Could Palestinians and Israelis finally join hands? Could some of us who struggle with addictions or with diseases that trap us be liberated by God and start to walk tall in the kingdom of God? When God descends to us at the end, could we perhaps awaken *every* day to "stabs of joy" in mornings "too full of beauty" for us?

If we believe in the kingdom of God we will pray, and we will hope for those without much hope left. We will drive through the fog of doubt that descends on even the keenest believers. (So sturdy a Puritan as Increase Mather wrote in his diary for July 29, 1664, that he was "grieved, grieved, grieved with temptations to Atheisme.")[3] And one more tough thing. We will work and study in the same direction as we hope. According to Lewis Smedes, hoping for others is hard, but not the hardest. Praying for others is hard, but not the hardest. The hardest task for people who believe in the second coming of Jesus Christ is in "living the sort of life that makes people say, 'Ah, so *that's* how people are going to live when righteousness takes over our world.'"[4]

The hardest task is simple, persistent faithfulness in our work

3. Michael G. Hall, *The Last American Puritan: The Life of Increase Mather, 1629-1723* (Middletown, CT: Wesleyan University Press, 1988), 65.

4. Smedes, *Standing on the Promises*, 173.

and in our attitudes — the kind of faithfulness that shows we are being drawn forward by the magnet force of the kingdom of God. Where learning is concerned, faithfulness means keeping at it long after a terminal degree. This means that even if you aren't thinking of pursuing graduate studies, your education ought never to end. Learning is a lifelong endeavor. That's why in one way it's not bad to think of your few years at Calvin as a process of "learning how to learn." As we've already seen, learning isn't just for self-fulfillment or career enhancement. We learn in order to throw ourselves into the battle for the kingdom of God.

And it *is* a battle. The kingdom of God is in ceaseless conflict with the kingdoms of this world. The kingdoms of the world, the flesh, and the devil oppose the kingdom of God with all the powers they can muster. Education for the sake of the kingdom isn't a wholly safe undertaking. A Christian who goes to work for the kingdom simultaneously goes to war. What's needed on God's side are well-educated warriors. We are now fallen creatures in a fallen world. The Christian gospel tells us that all hell has broken loose in this sad world and that, in Christ, all heaven has come to do battle. Christ has come to defeat the powers and principalities, to move the world over onto a new foundation, and to equip a people — informed, devout, determined people — to lead the way in righting what's wrong, in transforming what's corrupted, in doing the things that make for peace, expecting that these things will travel across the border from this world to the new heaven and earth.

That's what Christian higher education is for. That's what all Christian education is for. Seen at its broadest reach, Christian education is for the kingdom of God. Christian higher education equips us to be agents of the kingdom, models of the kingdom in our own lives and communities, witnesses to the kingdom wherever we go in the world. In a fallen world, Christian education is a powerful engine for ministering to the world along the same line that we hope for the world.

From time to time we do need to see this big picture of the kingdom of God in order to find our calling inside its frame. But day to day, the issues of good and evil will come to us undramatically. They will come to us in a score of small questions that test and reveal our commitment to God's will on earth. How do I spend my time? How do I spend my money? Why do so few of my good works really cost me something? How readily do I own up to messing up? How often do I think of Jesus Christ? How hard will I try to learn to spell and pronounce the name of an international student two doors down? When I daydream before falling asleep, whose happiness do I dream of?

Faithfulness in the small things can lead to faithfulness in the big things. What matters day by day is simple faithfulness to our calling, letting God decide the timetable for the great events, including the end of the human drama.

According to a story told by Os Guinness, an astute Christian social critic, the Connecticut House of Representatives was in session on a bright day in May, 1780, and the delegates were able to do their work by natural light. But then something happened that nobody expected. Right in the middle of debate, there was an eclipse of the sun and everything turned to darkness. Some of the legislators thought it was the Second Coming. So a clamor arose. People wanted to adjourn. People wanted to pray. People wanted to prepare for the coming of the Lord.

But the speaker of the House had a different idea and rose to the occasion with sound logic and good faith. We are all upset by the darkness, he said, and some of us are afraid. But, "the Day of the Lord is either approaching or it is not. If it is not, there is no cause for adjournment. And if the Lord *is* returning, I, for one, choose to be found doing my duty. I therefore ask that candles be brought."

And delegates who expected Jesus went back to their desks and resumed their debate.

Talking Points for Chapters 1 through 5

Chapter 1: Longing and Hope

- Agree or disagree: A person who didn't long for anything or anybody might be perfectly normal.
- What concrete steps might we take to expand our hopes for others?
- Why are peace and justice so often at the center of human hope?

Chapter 2: Creation

- If creation is in principle intelligible, does it follow that we ought to be able to explain it all? Scientists often study a particular life system with an eye on its possible contribution to *survival*. Would the discovery of survival value bring a Christian's search for intelligibility to its conclusion? Is survival value all that's interesting or significant about the way a created thing is put together?
- Paul says that corrupted human beings worship and serve "the creature rather than the Creator" (Rom. 1:25). Why is this a temptation?
- Genesis 1:27 has given some major theologians, including Karl

Barth (undoubtedly the greatest Protestant theologian of the last century), the idea that maleness and femaleness together constitute an image of God. Why might this idea be at least plausible?

- How is mockery a kind of treason? Why have scorn and mockery become a significant part of popular entertainment, and why do people find them entertaining? Why, at the same time, are people in real life hypersensitive to the possibility that somebody has disrespected them?

- Most Christians think that the normal state of human beings is that of "embodied souls" or "besouled bodies" ("normal," because 2 Corinthians 5:1-8 and Philippians 1:23-24 suggest that we can exist in union with Christ without our bodies, albeit in a sort of plucked and chilly condition). In any case, let's suppose that our bodies are a truly important part, but not the whole, of who we are. What follows with respect to how seriously we ought to take our bodies? Should a person with a low-quality body take it that she has a low-quality life? Should a person with a high-quality body take it that he has a high-quality life? What are the lines of really *healthy* thinking about our relation to our bodies?

Chapter 3: The Fall

- As we've seen, bad characters make for a bad culture, but a bad culture also makes for bad characters. Think of star athletes who curse each other and spit on referees. Are these athletes leaders or followers? Are they corrupting the appetites of their youthful fans, or are they simply giving a debased culture what it already wants?

- Richard Rorty, one of America's most famous contemporary philosophers, states that he couldn't become a Christian because he couldn't manage to confess his sins in prayer to God. He simply couldn't get himself to do that.[1] Why is confession of sin so difficult? What sin *makes* confession of sin so difficult?

1. Rorty, "There's No Big Picture," *University of Chicago Magazine,* April 1994, 20.

- Why does evil often look good to us, even exciting? Why do we find the story of a bank robbery more interesting than the story of a bank deposit?
- Suppose a roommate drives drunk and endangers himself and others. Suppose we know this is wrong and foolish. Should we confront him? Would that be judgmental? Would it be *thought* to be judgmental? If so, would that settle the question? Would it be more important to preserve our own reputation for tolerance than to preserve the safety of people we care about? Ephesians 4:15 suggests that "speaking the truth in love" is a mark of a spiritual grown-up, and Galatians 6:1 counsels us to correct each other "in a spirit of gentleness." Both verses suggest that rebuking each other is delicate surgery that needs to be done carefully. Where will we learn it? Suppose there is a time to speak and a time for silence (Eccles. 3:7). How do we know which is which?

Chapter 4: Redemption

- Genesis 3 narrates the fall by picturing human shame and divine grace. Since then, have human beings needed salvation from unhealthy forms of shame as well as from guilt? Are there healthy forms of shame? One popular form of North American entertainment consists of explicit revelations of people's affairs, divorces, sex-change surgeries, body-part augmentations, etc. Assuming something is objectionable about these instances of spilling the beans, what is it? Are the revelations shameful? Shameless? Merely tacky? What kind of redemption is needed by a person who reveals too much?
- In recent years, North American courts and school districts have quarreled over the question whether public schools may post the Ten Commandments. Despite understandable concerns by the courts that public schools ought not to favor a particular form of religion, schools have persisted in wanting to post the Commandments. Why so? What civic good might be achieved by posting the

Commandments? On the other hand, what significant part of their original context might get lost when the Commandments are displayed in secular settings?

- According to the Protestant reformers, salvation is by grace alone, through faith alone, in Christ alone. But if so, couldn't a person decide to coast? Couldn't a person decide to live however she wanted, thinking "I'm saved no matter what I do"? Alternatively, if we say that every regenerated person will certainly do good works and live a holy life — that, in fact, we can *tell* our faith by its fruits — won't we start anxiously introspecting? Won't we be tempted to fall back into the performance anxiety that God's grace is supposed to relieve?

- Given our differences in personal nature, and given our gender, racial, ethnic, and cultural differences, can the same rhythm of dying and rising sanctify us all? (Calvin called this rhythm "mortification and vivification.") Every day in India, a number of women are killed by husbands or fiancés because the woman's family didn't come up with a large enough dowry to please the killer. Even when permitted to live, women in many parts of the world are oppressed by daily humiliations intended to keep them in their place. If such women are, or become, Christians, must they still undergo the "mortification of their old nature"? Haven't they been mortified enough? Should a Christian missionary preach humility to people who have been humiliated for most of their lives?

  Calvin says that outside Christ we are trapped in a ceaseless oscillation between pride and despair. Do oppressors have more of the pride and victims more of the despair, so that when people die and rise with Christ they might start at different places? Should preachers and missionaries take this possibility into account, urging oppressors to repent and victims to hope in God? Or should preachers and missionaries preach exactly the same gospel, no matter who their audience is?

- In Romans 6 Paul writes that if you have died and risen with Christ you should "*consider* yourself dead to sin and alive to God."

Apparently a believer needs faith not only in Jesus Christ, but also in her own sanctification. Why might this faith be necessary? Why might believers sometimes need to give themselves the benefit of the doubt where their own spiritual condition is concerned?

Chapter 5: Vocation in the Kingdom of God

- If everything God has made is potentially redeemable (see Chapter 2), does the same go for everything human beings have made? Are there cultural products so corrupt that Christians have to forget about trying to redeem them and have to try instead to abolish them? On what basis? May Christians try to do this politically even if others complain that we are then "imposing our values" on them? Is that always wrong to do? If it's sometimes wrong, what makes it wrong? Don't all laws impose on somebody's values?
- Suppose that all worthy occupations may become part of our vocation. Are all occupations worthy? Are there some legal occupations that serious Christians could not accept because there isn't much chance of contributing to the kingdom in these occupations? Could a serious Christian be a casino dealer, for example? A pro boxing promoter? A manufacturer of a flammable combat jelly that sticks to human skin and can't be extinguished? A designer of video games that reward ruthlessness? A truly swanky fashion show coordinator? A manufacturer of dolls designed to look just like the children who love them, so that when children look at what they love they're looking at themselves?
- English Puritans, Dutch Calvinists, and many other Reformed Christians have developed a style of Christian faith that deliberately goes out to engage the world. "All of life is religious," they say. "Every square inch belongs to Jesus Christ." "There is no division between sacred and secular." Doesn't all this sound pretty worldly? What's to keep a Calvinist from slipping into mere social activism? If "reforming the cities" is just as Christian as going to church, why bother going to church?

- How may Christians believe in both "the antithesis" (the enduring battle between good and evil) and common grace? Don't we have to choose?
- A Christian who observes contemporary culture — contemporary entertainment culture, for example — will observe a bewildering mix of good and evil. She will find some healthy humor, but also some vile comedy. She will find a small amount of reverence, a small amount of overt blasphemy, and vast amounts of sheer, breezy indifference toward God. She will hear music that sounds like rebellion against creation and music that sounds like celebration of it. She will find scorn, cynicism, and an assumption to the effect that the pursuit of moral goodness is a quaint hobby of a few — perhaps something like stagecoach repair. She will also find, here and there and in unexpected places such as Hollywood, a film of such redemptive power (e.g., *Tender Mercies*) that it makes her weep.

Paul says, "hate what is evil, hold fast to what is good" (Rom. 12:9). But, as John Milton knew, "it was from out the rind of one apple tasted, that the knowledge of good and evil, as two twins cleaving together, leaped forth into the world."[2] How do you tell these twins apart? How do you *learn* to tell good from evil?

Milton says he doesn't trust a person's knowledge of goodness if that person hasn't gone out into the world to *test* his knowledge. A "cloistered virtue" doesn't help us. The point is that if we stay away from secular culture to protect ourselves from its temptations, we cannot live and witness in the real world. We can't even understand it.

But isn't there another side to this coin? Suppose we get close enough to secular culture to understand it, to witness to it, to try in some ways to reform it. How do we keep from being seduced by it?

---

2. Milton, "Areopagitica," in *Complete Poems and Major Prose,* ed. Merritt Y. Hughes (New York: Odyssey, 1957), 728.

APPENDIX II

Calvin College: An Historical Sketch[1]

When we hear the word "Reformation" as the description for an entire era in Western history, several images flash before the mind's eye. Surely one will be of Martin Luther standing before the door of Castle Church in Wittenberg, Germany, pounding a nail through the scroll of his Ninety-five Theses. While Luther intended to start a debate, not a movement, he catapulted the Western church into an era of perplexity, and he wasn't alone. Other theologians throughout Europe were already attempting to straighten the church's traditions with theological hammer blows of their own. Like Luther, they never intended, at least not at first, to form a "new" church, but to re-form the church they already served.

One such theologian was Ulrich Zwingli, whose movement begun in Switzerland soon earned the name "Reformed" because of its proposals, more radical than Luther's, for "re-forming" the church strictly according to the Word of God. Like Luther, the Swiss reformer hoped Scripture's teaching of "salvation by grace alone through faith in Christ" would become the basis of Christian faith and piety over against the Roman Church's teachings about works, but Zwingli went further than Luther in his doctrine of the church, its sacraments, and its organization.

1. Hearty thanks to Sue Rozeboom for authoring and Professor James Bratt for editing this short history.

Soon both Luther and Zwingli realized that the Roman Church couldn't be reformed from within, and that a new church should be established by those who protested its corruptions. In the process of defining that new church, Luther and Zwingli themselves parted company over disagreements about the Lord's Supper and the authority of Scripture. By clearly defining their theology on these and other points, setting it apart from both the Roman Catholic Church and other emerging Protestant churches, Zwingli and his followers established the "Reformed" churches around 1529. In 1531 Zwingli was killed in battle, and his work was left to his successors, one of whom was John Calvin.

Born in France, Calvin originally trained for a career in law. Shortly after earning his degree, he directed his studies toward Greek and Hebrew. During this time, in the late 1520s, Calvin was introduced to a reformatory movement in the church in France, a movement that derived from Luther. Calvin joined the movement about the same time that the King of France denounced it, declaring it anarchist and persecuting anyone associated with it. The bounty on Calvin's life was high, but in 1534 he managed a narrow escape to Basel, Switzerland. From there he sent a letter and an early draft of *The Institutes of the Christian Religion* to the King of France in defense of those who sought reform in the Roman Catholic Church. Realizing he couldn't return to France, at least not in the near future, Calvin sought a more permanent refuge. Because of his conviction that Scripture is the primary norm for faith and life, Calvin discovered a natural kinship with Zwingli's followers in Switzerland. Compelled by his convictions and his circumstances, Calvin took up his work in Geneva, where, among other things, he strove to establish a uniquely Christian civil society.

Having been highly educated himself, Calvin was convinced of the value of education in shaping Christians as better servants of God in church and society. Calvin maintained that an educational curriculum ought to include the works of believers and non-believers alike, since both may reveal beauty and truth and therefore merit our gratitude to God. For similar reasons, Calvin asserted that no discipline

> *"Whenever we come upon . . . secular writers, let that admirable light of truth shining in them teach us that the mind of man, though fallen and perverted from its wholeness, is nevertheless clothed and ornamented with God's excellent gifts. If we regard the Spirit of God as the sole fountain of truth, we shall neither reject the truth itself, nor despise it wherever it shall appear, unless we wish to dishonor the Spirit of God."*
>
> John Calvin[2]

should be excluded from a Christian academy and, like other reformers, claimed that every decent vocation ought to be engaged as service to God.[3] So nearly everywhere that Calvin's influence reached, two institutions were established: a church and a university.

Seeds of the "Reformed," or Calvinist, movement took root throughout Europe. Calvin College stems from the movement's growth in the Netherlands.

During the sixteenth century, Reformation ideas were tolerated in the Netherlands even though the rest of the Spanish Empire was intolerantly Catholic. Luther's ideas were trafficked from Germany, Zwingli's from Switzerland, and Calvin's from France and Geneva, with Calvin's clearly being the most influential in the long run.

In 1555 Philip II of Spain abruptly halted this free exchange. A zealous Roman Catholic and an even more zealous political sovereign, Philip enlisted the Spanish Inquisition to ferret out "heretics" of the Reformation in the Netherlands. Once discovered, Calvinists,

2. Calvin, *Institutes of the Christian Religion,* 1:273-74 (2.2.15).
3. Calvin, *Institutes,* 1:724-25 (3.11.6).

"I am shut up in the strongest and wretchedest of dungeons, so dark and gloomy that it goes by the name of the Black Hole. I can get but little air, and that of the foulest. I have on my hands and feet heavy irons which are a constant torture, galling the flesh even to my poor bones. But, notwithstanding all, my God fails not to make good His promise, and to comfort my heart, and to give me a most blessed content. . . . Your faithful husband, Guido de Brès, Minister of God's Word at Valenciennes, and at present prisoner for the Son of God."[4]

along with other Protestants — men, women, and children alike — were hung, burned, drowned, or buried alive. By 1570, the struggle of Protestants for religious freedom and the struggle of Netherlanders for political freedom essentially became one and the same struggle against Spain, a struggle that endured for eighty years.[5] By the end of

4. In Cornelius Plantinga, Jr., *A Place to Stand* (Grand Rapids: Board of Publications of the Christian Reformed Church, 1981), 35.

5. During this war, two of the Christian Reformed Church's confessions were written. Beginning in 1559 Guido de Brès circulated a confession, later known as the Belgic Confession, tossing one copy over Philip II's castle wall in 1562. As an outline of the Reformed faith, the Belgic Confession was meant to demonstrate that because Reformed believers were neither theological radicals nor political insurrectionists, the persecution should cease. De Brès was martyred in 1567. In 1618-1619, a Reformed synod convened in Dordrecht, Netherlands, to address the teachings of Jacobus Arminius and his followers. The Canons of Dort are an elucidation and refutation of Arminius's five points of doctrine. Contrary to Arminius, the synod affirmed the Reformed doctrines of Total Depravity, Unconditional Election, Limited Atonement, Irresistible Grace, and Perseverance of the Saints (TULIP).

the bloodshed, the Dutch had won their independence and the Reformed church had emerged as the preferred church in the state.

From there we fast-forward a century and a half to 1816. Soon after the collapse of Napoleon's continental campaign, the long-lived House of Orange was restored in the Netherlands. At that time, King Willem I reorganized the National Reformed Church of the Netherlands into the State Department of Religion. While this didn't mean that the National Church was the State Church (establishing a State Church would have violated the Enlightenment principle of religious toleration), it did mean that the National Reformed Church was supported with federal funds and privileged by the state. In effect, the Church had become a civic institution, a federal tool for promoting social unity rather than for stirring faith and shepherding believers.[6]

Laden with the state's Enlightenment ideals, the National Church soon yielded to a theological liberalism and spiritual coldness that was creeping across Europe. Many members found it unsavory. In 1834 these members seceded from the National Reformed Church, illegally, and so with a price: persecution was again visited to Reformed believers in the Netherlands. Among other things, the state outlawed their gatherings, quartered troops in their homes (in part to prevent secret meetings), imprisoned their preachers, and exacted exorbitant fines from their communities. Although a new king reversed these policies in 1840, residual misery, compounded by a severe economic depression, forced many to emigrate to North America in the second half of the decade.[7]

Upon arriving in the States, these Dutch immigrants received an invitation to join the Dutch Reformed Church, which had been established in New York in 1624. (Now named the Reformed Church in America, the Dutch Reformed Church treated the nineteenth-century Dutch immigrants hospitably, helping them find land for their colo-

---

6. James D. Bratt, *Dutch Calvinism in Modern America* (Grand Rapids: Eerdmans, 1984), 5. Also Michael Wintle, *Pillars of Piety: Religion in the Netherlands in the Nineteenth Century* (Hull: Hull University Press, 1987), 11ff.

7. Bratt, *Dutch Calvinism,* 7-9.

nies and offering them seed money for churches and schools, including Hope College.) In 1850, Albertus C. Van Raalte — who had founded Holland, Michigan, with several hundred other immigrants — accepted their offer. In so doing he perturbed many, especially those who immigrated to the colony between 1850 and 1857. They were anxious about this North American version of the Dutch Reformed Church, which reminded them of the liberal church they had left in the Netherlands: their theology seemed lax; they sang not just Psalms, but hymns, too; and they permitted lodge membership.

So in 1857 four congregations — three from the Holland area and one from Grand Rapids — seceded from the Dutch Reformed Church (again, you could say) and soon established what it called the True Dutch Reformed Church. Adopting the title "true" might seem a little audacious, but it was meant to be a beacon for future immigrants, a sign of who was who among Dutch believers in North America. It wasn't until 1890 that the "true" church became the "Christian Reformed" church, now the Christian Reformed Church in North America.

A generation passed and the new immigrant communities were growing rapidly. More and more churches were being built, but there weren't enough ministers to fill these pulpits. Since ministers in the Netherlands couldn't be encouraged to cross the ocean to serve a church that the Christian Reformed Church in the Netherlands didn't officially recognize, it became clear that qualified men in the North American community needed to be trained for ministry. (The Christian Reformed Church has only recently opened ordained ministry to women.)

Members of the True Dutch Reformed Church expected their ministers to be highly educated, having a solid understanding of the church and its history, the Reformed faith and its theology, and the Bible and its Reformed interpretation. To provide a proper education for its ministers, the True Dutch Reformed Church established in Grand Rapids what it called the Theological School and appointed Reverend Gerrit Boer as its sole professor.

Reverend Boer took up his duties on February 18, 1876. His classroom was anything but serene: he and his seven students met on the second floor of Williams Street Christian Elementary School, located next to the Grand Rapids train yard. Grinding engine noise and piercing train whistles provided ample competition for the professor's concentration and the students' attention. And the seven students were anything but "traditional" (by today's standards, that is). Plucked from the seats of milk delivery wagons and horse-drawn plows, most of Boer's first students were academically fortified only with the grammar-school education that they had received years before. For them, memorizing verb conjugations in Hebrew, Greek, Latin, and German and wrestling with theology in these languages were unusual chores.

In time the school grew and Reverend Boer's teaching load was somewhat relieved by the addition of more professors. By the mid-1890s the Theological School had relocated to the corner of Franklin and Madison, where students and professors enjoyed spacious classrooms and decreased noise pollution. Around the same time, the school's Literary Department — essentially a preparatory program in languages for students who wished to become ministers — broadened in scope and purpose. Those who anticipated vocations other than ministry, such as teaching in the Christian schools, were also admitted, a policy that paved the way for establishing a college. Still, it was not until 1902 that non-seminary students, including women, began to enroll in any significant numbers.

Debate mounted in the church about whether a college should be spawned from the preparatory programs of the Theological School. Progress was slow and carefully planned by those who wanted a college, many of whom were recent immigrants who had been influenced by Abraham Kuyper's reform movement in the Netherlands at the turn of the century. Finally in the fall of 1907, students were able to enroll in a two-year program at what was called the John Calvin Junior College. By 1910 the two-year program had blossomed into a three-year program, for which students paid $26.00 a year for tuition.

Throughout the 1910s, enrollment in the junior college and the Theological School continued to increase despite the outbreak of

> *"Let us remember we are building not so much for the present but for the future; we build not so much for ourselves but for the coming generations. . . . This proposed College is not the hobby of a few; it is the most serious thing that has come up as yet in the history of our Church and people. Let us not throw away our chance of beginning to build up a College . . . in fulfilling our calling to the glory of the triune God."*
>
> B. K. Kuiper[8]

World War I. As quarters became more and more cramped, church and school officials prepared for a second move. Having investigated offers of land and seed money from Kalamazoo, Muskegon, and Grand Rapids, officials purchased a plot of land in a healthy residential section of Grand Rapids on Franklin Street near Fuller Avenue. In 1916 construction crews laid the cornerstone of the administration building, which was occupied by the college and seminary within the following year.

By this time the three-year junior college program was on a fast track toward becoming a fully accredited four-year program, a status it achieved by the fall of 1920. In June of 1921 eight men received their baccalaureate diplomas with hopes of teaching, doing graduate work, or taking up careers in law or business. Fourteen others were planning to continue course work at Calvin's Theological School.

Though only newly born, Calvin College had a strong foundation and good reason to hope the best for its future. The student body was

8. B. K. Kuiper, *The Proposed Calvinistic College at Grand Rapids* (Grand Rapids: B. Sevensma, 1903), 65.

> *"Not by might of human intellect we do this, not by power of human invention, but by God's Spirit blessed forevermore."*
>
> Dr. Henry Beets, Address on the Occasion of the Laying of the Corner Stone, Calvin College, June 22, 1916[9]

steadily growing; the Christian Reformed Church was financially supportive; the facilities were new and there was promise of expanding them. The president of the college, Reverend J. J. Hiemenga, had lofty goals, saying he intended Calvin to be strong enough to "compete with any institution of its kind."[10] This wasn't a boast, but a vow: Calvin College, in her work carried out before the face of God, would put forth only her best. But many in the church were convinced that Hiemenga's statement was a grim foreshadowing of the college's slippage into "worldliness."

Above everything, worldliness was perceived to be the single greatest threat to the faith of a believer and the life of the church. Members of the Christian Reformed Church did everything they could imagine to hold it at bay, which is one reason why many of these first and second generation immigrants refused to be influenced by North American culture. But World War I invaded their anxious isolation, a circumstance that some in the Christian Reformed Church welcomed and others feared.

The delicate tension that existed between these two groups was not new. As the college emerged in the early 1900s, so did two distinct points of view over its nature and purpose. On the one side were those

9. *The Banner* 51 (June 29, 1916): 422.
10. "Our Own Calvin," *Calvin Annual, 1920* (Grand Rapids: Calvin College, 1920), 30.

who were sensitive to the threat of worldliness and keenly aware of the "antithesis" that exists between this world and the kingdom of God. While such folk were grateful to be living in a free country, they were afraid of the darker side of that freedom, and even more afraid of how it might influence young people. They were eager to establish a "safe place" for the sons and daughters of the Christian Reformed Church to study, and to them, "safe" meant a school wholly separate from the unbelieving professors and partying students of America's secular universities; "safe" meant a curriculum saturated with biblical studies and Reformed doctrine.[11]

On the other side were those who were eager to establish a college where students and professors would not flee from the world as a cautionary measure against worldliness. Rather, they would responsibly *engage* the world — every dimension of it — in hope of bettering it. Such people were eager to find the good in culture and society, to cause it to flourish, and by that flourishing to redeem what had gone wrong.[12]

But this was the 1920s, an era historians have dubbed "The Roaring 20s," and with good reason. A moral revolution — some might say a moral "devolution" — was underway in America as traditional values were displaced by the matured views of Darwin, Freud, and Marx on the one hand, and by the raciness of contemporary culture's bootlegged booze, jazz, dancing, and tabloid papers on the other. So it's relatively easy to understand why many church and college leaders chose to avoid American culture rather than to engage it. In 1928, the governing body of the Christian Reformed Church denounced "three worldly amusements": dancing, card-playing, and theatre-attendance.[13] At the same meeting, they deposed a Calvin seminary

11. James Bratt and Ronald Wells, "Piety and Progress: A History of Calvin College," in *Keeping Faith: Embracing the Tensions in Christian Higher Education* (Grand Rapids: Eerdmans, 1996), 26.
12. Professor B. K. Kuiper was among the first to articulate such a vision for Calvinists in America. See John J. Timmerman, *Promises to Keep: A Centennial History of Calvin College* (Grand Rapids: Eerdmans, 1975), 36 and 47.
13. *Acta Synodi, 1928* (Grand Rapids: Christelijke Gereformeerde Kerk, 1928), 88.

> *"Scripture not only teaches us about the way of salvation but sheds light on great world problems. Even more, it does not place these two, the way of salvation and natural life, next to each other as in two ticket-lines but intertwines them and offers us a view of the world, its origin, its historical course, and its destiny in which the entire work of redemption fits as in an invisible matrix. With these fixed points in front of us, we are afforded the possibility of constructing an entire Christian scholarship that frees us from idle speculation and gives us knowledge of the real condition of things, as it was, and is, and shall be."*
>
> Abraham Kuyper[14]

professor, B. K. Kuiper, who admitted he attended an occasional movie in order "to understand the American people." Since he reneged on a promise that he wouldn't go again, the church dismissed him.[15]

Given its fear of worldliness, the church wasn't concerned merely with what professors and students did during their spare time. Church officials were also concerned with the courses of study that were offered at the college. They suspected certain fields (such as art, philosophy, and science) because of their reputation for being especially open to secular influence in the American academy. So, though

14. Abraham Kuyper, "Common Grace in Science," in *Abraham Kuyper: A Centennial Reader,* ed. James Bratt (Grand Rapids: Eerdmans, 1998), 459-60.

15. Timmerman, *Promises,* 37; *Acta Synodi, 1928* (Grand Rapids: Christelijke Gereformeerde Kerk, 1928), 84/190.

these programs eventually flourished at Calvin, their development was watched closely during the 1920s and 30s.

While church officials were busy keeping Calvin's faculty in line, the faculty were responsible for keeping students in line, inside and outside the classroom. This meant catching students who indulged in pranks, "worldly amusements," or other raucous behaviors, such as fistfights and vandalism after Calvin-Hope basketball games.

The Calvin-Hope men's basketball rivalry tipped off in 1921. After six games (all of which Hope won), college officials blew their whistles for a three-year time-out because the competition was too intense for coaches, players, and especially fans. Since then, the otherwise friendly rivalry in men's basketball has endured two more cooling off periods, 1936-1942 and 1944-1945. In other men's and women's sports, the rivalry has simply remained friendly, with Hope and Calvin teams often just besting one another.

All the early concern about protecting the college from worldliness came to a head in 1939. In that year, faculty papers and course syllabi were scrutinized by the governing body of the church, which harbored fierce suspicions about the college's academic activity. Disappointed with student conduct (or at least with what was rumored) and the faculty's management of it, the same governing body compelled students to sign pledge cards, hoping to bind their consciences — not surprisingly — against dancing, playing cards, and seeing movies. The pledge cards were dismissed in 1949; the church blessed film as a "legitimate cultural medium" in 1966;[16] and the college allowed so-called "foot-functions" and "parties with music" in the 1970s, and sponsored campus-wide dances in the 1980s.

It's easy to smile at this drama. But the earlier generations wrestled with real questions: How are we to love God and then live honestly by that love? How do we engage culture without immersing ourselves in it? How do we immerse ourselves in it without *losing* ourselves in it? What exactly is the right posture of a Christian who

---

16. "The Church and the Film Arts," *Acts of Synod, 1966* (Grand Rapids: CRC Publications, 1966), 339.

wants to be "in the world, but not of it"? Around Calvin, such questions have generated a perpetual examination of "responsible freedom" and "the integration of faith with learning."[17]

From this description of Calvin's early history, one might get the idea that Calvin was so involved in discipline that little else was accomplished. Actually, the college expanded significantly during the 1920s and 30s. Despite the economic depression of the early 30s, the number of students at Calvin more than doubled, from 220 in 1920 to 520 in 1941. The student body was small, but student clubs were abundant, most of them academic in focus. When clubs like Pierian explored great literature or Philoi Aletheias discussed philosophy, rooms filled with smoke as much from heated debate as from puffed cigars. *Chimes,* which marked its 25th year in print in 1932, had already become a lively forum for reporting campus activity and venting student opinion. Movies were anathema, but stage productions weren't, so Thespians (now the Calvin Theatre Company) enjoyed a fairly enthusiastic welcome when they stepped onto the scene in 1932. The music department was thriving by that time too, largely due to the efforts of Professor Seymour Swets. Courses were added in the social sciences, and several more in the natural sciences.

By this time Calvin was beginning to receive national attention, too, in part because of the contributions of William Harry Jellema, a renowned professor of philosophy. In Calvin's community, his love of God and love of truth and love of a sound argument — and his rigorous pursuit of these loves in the classroom — deeply influenced colleagues and students for years to come. These included H. Evan Runner (despite his disagreements with Jellema) and Henry Zylstra in one generation, and Alvin Plantinga and Nicholas Wolterstorff in the next.

But this rapid rate of activity couldn't be sustained in the early 1940s, not with America's involvement in World War II. Enrollment declined slightly, hovering near 500 students for most of the war. Not

---

17. President Henry Schultze coined this phrase in the Calvin community in the 1940s (Timmerman, *Promises,* 95ff.).

surprisingly, most of these students were women. A few faculty and several students were drafted into the Armed Services, some never to return. Courses were cut, but clubs and extracurricular programs continued to thrive: students on campus joined these groups to honor former members who had been called up for service. Along with the rest of the world, Calvin waited for peace.

When the war in Europe ended in the spring of 1945, Calvin was comfortably educating and housing 503 students — three more students than its capacity. But in the fall of 1945, Calvin admitted an astonishing 1,245 students, many of whom were veterans. In order to accommodate them, the college invested in army surplus. A reconstructed mess hall on the west lawn of the Franklin Street campus provided space for science classes and music rehearsals. Recently declared unsafe for children, a nearby elementary school building was outfitted with army surplus bunks, cots, and foot lockers for student housing.

Obviously these arrangements could be only temporary. A successful fund-raising campaign yielded enough resources to begin construction on a science building, a dining hall, and an addition to the library. President Henry Schultze and the Board of Trustees worked hard to hire more professors, but qualified candidates who shared the college's vision of "integrated, God-centered" education were few at the time, so it took more than ten years for the student/faculty ratio to level off.

> *". . . the greatest idea about Calvin College is an intangible and an invisible one. It is the idea on which Calvin College was founded in 1876 and the idea on which it still exists in 1954. That idea is a dynamic faith in a living God."*
>
> *Prism, 1954*

While the threat of Communism loomed large in the West during the 1950s (this was the decade of the Korean conflict, Castro's ascendancy in Cuba, and the Army-McCarthy hearings in the United States), Calvin quietly prospered. Enrollment steadily increased: nearly 2,000 students registered for classes in 1960. In order to handle the rising activity on campus, Dr. William Spoelhof, who succeeded Dr. Henry Schultze as president in 1951, gradually expanded the staff and administration. But that only increased the college's need for more *space.*

Under Dr. Spoelhof's superintendency the college moved from the Franklin Street campus to its current campus, the "Knollcrest" campus. Though hard for the college's leaders to plot at the time, the move actually began in 1954, when the President and the Board of Trustees decided not to initiate any new building projects on the Franklin Street campus so that they could determine which would be wiser: to stay in the neighborhood where the college currently existed or to move to a larger piece of land on the edge of town. If the college stayed, expansion would always be a problem since facilities were landlocked by residential properties and a city park; if the college purchased a large piece of land outside of town, it would be able to develop its facilities freely. Needless to say, college officials decided to move, but the decision didn't come easily.

One major reason for the difficulty was that many in Calvin's community were committed to the life of the city. They didn't wish to flee its looming social tensions by moving, but to engage them with a strong voice of reconciliation. By the time the college actually started to move in the 1960s, many more in Calvin's community had become disillusioned with the college's decision to leave the Franklin Street campus. Racial turmoil was escalating throughout the United States. Communities everywhere, including Grand Rapids, witnessed "white flight" from "changing" neighborhoods. So for many, the decision to move further away from the inner city seemed to betray the college's mission.[18]

18. Bratt and Wells, "Piety," 32; Timmerman, *Promises,* 144ff.

In 1956 church officials approved the purchase of the Knollcrest estate, a 166-acre farm on a dusty gravel road on the southeast side of Grand Rapids. An architectural firm in Chicago was hired to design the new campus, and William Fyfe, a student of Frank Lloyd Wright, was assigned to be its master planner. In order to inspire Fyfe's design, President Spoelhof submitted documents that outlined the philosophy of the college as a whole and described the purpose of each building that would be constructed.[19] If there was one overriding principle for the design of Calvin's campus, it was this: that Calvin College is a community of scholars in which academic departments, student services, and administrative divisions serve the educational mission equally. That's why no building or department is the "center" of Calvin's campus, but a large communal lawn is. Along with that, both the college and the architect were intent on preserving the natural beauty of Knollcrest farm by leaving its gentle slopes undisturbed. So buildings assume the contour of the land, which is why you might enter a building on the third floor at one end, and exit that building from the second floor at the other.

The seminary building across the pond was completed and occupied in 1960; the library and Hiemenga Hall in 1962. By 1963 the college community was split between two campuses. Administrative offices were located on both campuses, and both campuses held mandatory chapel services. First-year students lived in the residence halls and ate in Knollcrest Dining Hall on the new campus. Most of their courses were taught in Hiemenga Hall. If one of their classes was offered at the Franklin Street campus, a wheezing school bus would shuttle them there. After the Fieldhouse, the Fine Arts Center, and four more residence halls were completed by 1966, the sophomores moved to the new campus, too. The Commons and Science Building were finished in 1968, when enrollment peaked at 3,575 students. Finally, in 1973 the college marked the end of its move with the completion of the College Center, which now bears President Spoelhof's name.

19. Timmerman, *Promises*, 119. See also Bratt and Wells, "Piety," 37.

"The Christian mind as the mind with which we think and evaluate and choose and believe and hope is more important than isolated opinions that we think or learn. . . . Christianity means 'antithesis' . . . to make the 'antithesis' articulate, to make it concrete, to make it more than merely verbal, to make it mean more than simply insisting on our occupying a separate suite in the same mansions of modernity, we must know the objective minds of paganism and modernity."

William Harry Jellema[20]

Relocating the college was a long and arduous task, but it wasn't the only challenge that the college faced during the 1960s. While many Americans, including some at Calvin, rallied beneath the slogan "make love, not war" to initiate social revolution and to stand against America's involvement in the Vietnam War, the college rallied beneath Professor William Harry Jellema's critique of Calvin's curriculum to revolutionize its academic programming. Faculty were eager to develop a curriculum that would be seriously Christian, academically excellent, and culturally relevant, all and at once.[21] Recognizing that the current curriculum had been basically adopted from the secular university with a few religion and theology courses tacked on, faculty hoped to define a curriculum that would be uniquely fitting for a Reformed Christian liberal arts college. Work on the new curriculum began in 1963. After five years of debate, the college finally set-

20. William Harry Jellema, *The Curriculum in a Liberal Arts College: A Study More Immediately in the Context of Calvin College* (Grand Rapids: Calvin College, 1958), 25-26.
21. Timmerman, *Promises*, 167ff.

tled on a plan entitled *Christian Liberal Arts Education*, written primarily by Professor Nicholas Wolterstorff. The goal of the plan for Christian higher education was, and is, familiar enough: "teachers and students together engaging in the various scholarly disciplines, directed and enlightened in their inquiries by the Word of God."[22] What was fresh was the focus on the disciplines and how the curriculum of each would be affected by this plan. Other new features included the January interim and the larger number of core courses all students would take.

Keenly interested in the cultural relevance of their education, students during the 1960s arranged a few courses of their own, so to speak. Top on their list of issues to discuss were race relations, the war in Vietnam, and the degradation of the environment. Guest speakers, some of whom aroused significant controversy, were invited to address each of these issues. Groups of students traveled hundreds of miles to participate in peaceful protests: in 1964 several headed to Selma, Alabama, for a civil rights march, and in 1967 others drove to Washington, D.C., for an anti-war demonstration at the Pentagon. In the fall of 1969 the Student Senate petitioned the Faculty Senate for a suspension of campus activity so that students, faculty, and staff might engage in an "academic discussion of the moral aspects of the war" in Vietnam.[23] On October 15 several hundred gathered in the Knollcrest Fieldhouse for a two-hour presentation followed by a silent march across campus. In the spring of that same school year the college ceased activity again, this time for a teach-in on the environment as part of a nationwide observation of Earth Day.

The biggest headache Dr. Spoelhof endured during his presidency was caused by a student prank in 1970. Just as they do now, the *Chimes* staff then printed a mock issue of a publication familiar to the Calvin community. In 1970 they satirized *The Banner*, the magazine of

22. Nicholas Wolterstorff, *Christian Liberal Arts Education* (Grand Rapids: Calvin College and William B. Eerdmans, 1970), 47.

23. "Senate proposal rejected; faculty accepts compromise," *Chimes,* 10 October 1969. See also "Peace service, city rally, highlight Calvin Moratorium activity," *Chimes,* 17 October 1969.

the Christian Reformed Church. *Chimes'* version, *The Bananer* (adorned on each page with a tiny banana logo), drew enraged responses from hundreds in the church, many of whom barraged President Spoelhof's office with letters of disappointment. Disciplinary action was taken, but expulsion of the student editors withheld. (Three of them are now highly respected professors or administrators at Calvin.) The passing of this storm marked the end of an era: except for *The Bananer,* the 70s were quiet compared to the 60s.

Just as the college completed its move to the Knollcrest campus in the early 1970s, it also suffered a drop in student enrollment. The situation was a wake-up call for college officials: Calvin needed to be more active in identifying and recruiting prospective students, especially those from outside the Christian Reformed Church. While there had always been some students of other church backgrounds at Calvin, the 70s marked the beginning of greater denominational diversity on campus. Along with it came a commitment to increase racial diversity on campus, too, among students, faculty, and administration. Gains may seem small, but the commitment remains strong.

Along with these changes in the student body came significant changes in Calvin's Student Life Division. Formerly, students in campus housing were overseen by older women, most of whom were widows. It wasn't until the 1970s that professionals in relevant fields were appointed as Deans and Resident Directors. Even the college chaplain was a fairly new face on Calvin's campus, the first, Reverend Bernard Pekelder, having been appointed in the mid-60s.

Calvin's academic programming expanded during the early 70s, too. While college officials wanted to keep Calvin's program from becoming "career training" at the expense of broad exposure to the liberal arts, they did want to open Calvin's doors to professional programs that fit within the college's mission.[24] Some programs already existed, at least in part: teacher education, engineering, nursing, and

24. Richard Mouw, principal author for the Calvin College Professional Programs Committee, "Professional Education and the Christian Liberal Arts College," February 9, 1973.

business.[25] As a result of the more recent study, new programs in accounting, criminal justice, recreation, and social work were eventually introduced. Today, more students graduate with degrees in professional and pre-professional programs than with general degrees in the humanities or sciences.

At the beginning of the college's centennial year, Dr. William Spoelhof retired. Having been president for twenty-five years, he held the office longer than any of Calvin's presidents, before or since, and gave the college enduring and resourceful leadership. In fact, it would be exceedingly difficult to take the full measure of this man's stature in the history of Calvin College. In anticipation of his retirement, the Board of Trustees appointed a presidential search committee, which recommended two men for the position: Dr. Nicholas Wolterstorff, Professor of Philosophy at Calvin College, and Dr. Anthony Diekema, Associate Chancellor and Associate Professor of Medical Education at the University of Illinois Medical Center. Perhaps hoping to hold Wolterstorff and to acquire Diekema, the governing body of the church elected Dr. Diekema, whom the college inaugurated in the spring of 1976.

Among other things, President Diekema was keenly interested in enhancing the professional opportunities of faculty at Calvin, which in turn would enhance the academic activities of students. Soon after he became president, Diekema instituted grants that would allow more faculty to take sabbaticals for research and writing. He also enthusiastically supported the opening of the Calvin Center for Christian Scholarship in 1977, a project spearheaded by President Spoelhof several years earlier. Early CCCS projects focused on examining contemporary issues "through the eyes of faith." Scholars from various disciplines formed research teams, many of which held a conference or published a book based on their work. Professors at Calvin contributed to nearly all of these projects, along with Christian scholars from colleges and universities around the world.

25. Until the 1980s, only the first three years of an engineering program could be taken at Calvin, and the B.S. in nursing degree came in the 80s.

In the mid-80s, the college was rocked with controversy again. Three science professors, Clarence Menninga, Howard Van Till, and Davis Young, were investigated because of their published analysis of the origin of the world and their apparent leanings in the creation/evolution debate. In the end, after the college and the Christian Reformed Church had examined the issues thoroughly, all three professors were exonerated. The college and the church agreed that the scientists' inquiries were acceptable in the light of Reformed faith and useful in the context of a Christian academic community.[26]

In 1989 the college chapel was completed. Many considered this to be the final chapter of Calvin's move from the Franklin campus since its construction (though not this exact design) had always been included in the original master plan. At the urging of many students and some college officials, mandatory chapel had been abandoned in 1971. Though the enthusiasm of faculty and students for daily chapel has waxed and waned ever since it was instituted in 1900 (when

> *"What I want to nurture in my classroom is faith, taken both as a noun and as a verb. As a noun, faith is the Christian faith, . . . a body of beliefs as well as that vital component of redeemed experience granted by God's grace. As a verb, faith embraces faithfulness, the living out of salvation in the totality of life."*
>
> Susan M. Felch[27]

26. *Acts of Synod, 1988* (Grand Rapids: CRC Publications, 1988), 385-87, 591-99. See also Malcolm McBryde, "Creation: That 'Elegant Book,'" *The Banner* 123 (27 June 1988), 8-9.

27. Susan M. Felch, "Wise Doubters and Truth Seekers," a tenure review essay published in *Spark* 45, no. 1 (Spring 1999): 23.

compulsory services were at 7:45 a.m.), the program today enjoys the lively participation of hundreds of faculty, staff, and students each week.

The early 1990s were marked by a $35 million fund-raising campaign to enlarge Calvin's endowment. In the end, generous donors had contributed $50 million to support new construction projects, student scholarships, and endowed faculty chairs. The college is still reaping the benefits of that successful campaign, and, thankfully, its momentum hasn't been lost.

After 20 years of service, Dr. Diekema retired in 1996, and Dr. Gaylen Byker — a man of extraordinarily wide-ranging gifts and interests — was appointed to the office of President. The college continues to grow as it serves more than 4,200 students representing more than 75 ethnicities, national and international. Facilities continue to expand, on both sides of the Beltline and even off campus. Since the first was commissioned on Lake Drive in 1997, two more Project Neighborhood houses have been set up in the inner city. There, students live in intentional community and let their hospitality to one another overflow to their neighbors. These houses, along with the hundreds of other Service-Learning projects that take place in the heart of the city every year, are marks of the college's commitment to a community it seemed to have left some thirty years ago.

> *"Peniel means 'face of God.' We want this house to reflect the face of God to our neighbors. As we build relationships and learn what it means to become true neighbors, we pray that this house, the Peniel House, might represent the love, grace, power, and mercy of the living God throughout this neighborhood."*
>
> Peniel House Residents, January 2001

In the fall of 2000, the college revised its core curriculum again. Why again? To provide students with a fresh education that is seriously Christian, academically excellent, and culturally relevant, all and at once; an education that explores not just academic disciplines, but the whole world, as seen through the eyes of disciplined faith. For the whole world is the real world, and the real world is an arena for service to the kingdom of God. Through the learning that takes place here, we seek to be agents of renewal, to offer our hearts and lives to do God's work in God's world.

> *"To be human is to be that place in creation where God's goodness is meant to find its answer in gratitude. . . . learning is an act of gratitude to God. Most of you will know that the Greek word for thanksgiving is eucharistia. . . . learning is a eucharistic act."*
>
> Nicholas Wolterstorff[28]

28. Nicholas Wolterstorff (with thanks to Brian Gerrish), "The Standing of the Work of Our Hands," in *Keeping Faith: Embracing the Tensions in Christian Higher Education* (Grand Rapids: Eerdmans, 1996), 140.

An Engagement with God's World: The Core Curriculum of Calvin College

A STATEMENT OF PURPOSE

Adopted by the Calvin College Faculty
November 3, 1997
March 15, 1999
April 5, 1999

Ad hoc Core Curriculum Committee	Educational Policy Committee
Cheryl Kreykes Brandsen	Joel Carpenter, Provost
Ken Bratt	Andrea DeKoter
Jeanette Bult DeJong (1996-1998)	David Diephouse, Chair
Steve Chang (1996-1997)	Susan Felch
Susan Felch	David Laverell
Lee Hardy, Chair	William Stevenson
Douglas Howard	Michael Stob
Jeremy Konyndyk	Gloria Goris Stronks
John Lee (1997-1998)	Steven Timmermans
Cornelius Plantinga, Jr.	Steven Vander Leest
Richard Plantinga	
Steven Timmermans	
David Van Baak (1996-1998)	
Matthew Walhout (1998-1999)	

Appendix III

Preface

Among the many pieces of advice given in the literature on general education re-form, two stand out as both sound and of particular relevance to the formulation of a statement of purpose for the core curriculum. One is that, before embarking on any reform or revision of its general education program, an institution should be clear about the purpose of general education. The second is that the purpose of a general education program should be fitted to an institution's understanding of its particular mission as shaped by its tradition. These points are well taken, and so we preface the statement of purpose for the core curriculum with a brief reflection on Calvin's mission and identity.

The Christian Mission of Calvin College

Of the several formulations of educational mission to be found in Calvin's *Expanded Statement of Mission,* none is more succinct or more precise than the following: "Calvin College seeks to engage in vigorous liberal arts education that promotes lives of Christian service" (ESM, p. 33). The distinctive feature of this mission is not vigorous liberal arts education; for hundreds of institutions of higher education across the North American continent are engaged in that very project. Nor is it to be found in the promotion of lives of service; for many schools are likewise engaged. Rather, it is the combination of these two elements under the heading of "Christian."

The distinguishing mark of the mission of Calvin College derives, like all Christian missions, from Jesus Christ, the Son of God, the king of creation, the savior of all who place their trust in him. For the Christian life, including the Christian academic life, centers on the person of Christ — on his incarnation, life, death, resurrection, and ascension, and on the sovereign love that these astounding events express. Christians seek to live their whole lives in continuity with Christ, taking on his mind and affections, acting as his body in the world, sharing his sufferings and his victories in the project of overcoming human misery and rebuilding God's good creation. Chris-

178

tians gladly join this project out of gratitude to Christ, out of obedience to Christ, and out of an enkindled desire to work within the Kingdom of Christ. As faithful workers within this Kingdom, Christians struggle to align themselves with the redemptive purposes of God in this world, daily mortifying their evil desires and vivifying their good desires. Those who have "died and risen with Christ" in their baptism try to keep this rhythm going throughout their lives.

Thus Christians learn to shun what is evil and to cling to what is good. In so doing, however, they also learn how often good and evil are twisted around each other, so that each seems to grow out of the other, generating the great ironies and mysteries that fill the history of our world. They learn how often we deceive ourselves about where real good and evil lie, and how such deception dulls and distorts our grasp of reality. Indeed, given the power, scope, and deeply ingrown nature of sin, Christians develop a sense that the life God asks of us often goes against the grain of our resident desires and common assumptions. For that reason we are constantly tempted to make a small thing of the Christian life, to limit it to a modest portion of our beliefs and a narrow slice of our attitudes and behavior.

Faithfulness to Christ, then, includes a kind of wariness where our own judgment of good and evil is concerned, together with a readiness to submit it to the clarifying revelation of Scripture. Reformed Christians take seriously the corrupting force of sin, and therefore lay heavy emphasis upon the need to reform our lives and our view of life according to the incorruptible Word of God. But Reformed Christians also take seriously the renewing power of God's grace, released in human hearts and human societies by the Spirit of God, and they spot signs of this grace wherever they live. In fact, they come to see all of life and culture under the sway of Jesus Christ and as the sphere of faithful obedience to him. They realize that no part of God's fallen creation is left out of God's redemptive intent. This wide view of our life's arena and call, corrected by the lens of God's Word, is what some of our Reformed forebears meant when they spoke of the need to adopt a "Christian world-and-life view." In the Reformed tradition, Christian education is not just education as usual with Bible classes tacked on; it is an education that is permeated throughout by a Christian view of the world. In the Reformed tradition, the life of Christian service is not limited just to the church and its missions; it is found in every vocation where God's creative and redemptive purposes are pursued. In the Reformed tradition of liberal arts education, the whole life of the mind combines with the whole life of service under the headship of Christ.

The Reformed Identity of Calvin College

Calvin College is an academy rooted in the Reformed Christian tradition. Its educational mission is profoundly shaped by this tradition, a tradition woven of many strands, chief among which are the historical, theological, and practical. Taken together, these strands constitute the main lineaments of Calvin's Reformed identity.

The Historical Strand

While it is natural to think of the origins of Reformed Christianity as residing in the Reformation of the sixteenth century, the theological sources of the Reformed tradition are to be found much earlier than the celebrated year of 1517. The Protestant quarrel with Rome, after all, did not concern the parameters of orthodoxy as defined by the Patristic tradition of the Christian church — most notably in the ecumenical creeds and the doctrines of God and Christ they express — but rather the abuses of power and authority rife in the church of the day. Luther's Ninety-Five Theses were intended to initiate a debate about indulgences and the allied doctrine of justification, not the nature of God or Christ. After much conflict and a growing estrangement from the hierarchy of the Roman Church, Luther became ever more firmly convinced that ultimate authority in matters of faith could not be vested in the pope or the tradition but in holy scripture alone, a most ancient source.

As Luther and his followers came to the conclusion that an inner reform of the church was impossible, they also understood that their departure from Roman Catholic Christianity entailed the daunting task of giving a full and independent articulation to their newfound theological understandings. This articulation would be in part an appropriation of the tradition from which they came, in part a rejection of that same tradition. For they owned its orthodoxy, but rejected its errors and excesses. Born in reaction to the abuses of the church, Protestant Christianity would soon acquire its own set of distinctive emphases: the primary authority of the Word of God as presented in scripture (minus the deuterocanonical books) and all that seemed to follow from this central principle, including a liturgy centered on the sermon, a revised theology of the sacraments, and an emphasis on salvation by grace alone through faith alone.

By the time John Calvin, Ulrich Zwingli, and the second generation of reformers began their work in the cause, serious disputes had broken out among the Protestants themselves. The Reformed theological task then consisted not only of self-identification over against the Roman Church but also against other wings of Protestantism. In the subsequent development of Calvinist thought and practice, which came to be called Reformed in Switzerland and eventually beyond its borders, the articulation of identity was thus initially and for the most part negative: Reformed Christians were not Roman Catholics, Lutherans, or Anabaptists insofar as they differed with these Christian communities on a number of theological points.

But the religious identity of Reformed Christians was only proximately rooted in the work of Calvin and the teachings of the Protestant Reformation. Ultimately, it was anchored in Christian orthodoxy as delivered to the church in the Patristic period. Hence, as their faith and practice spread from Switzerland to other parts of Europe, Reformed Christians came in time to articulate their identity in more positive terms and with lasting significance on the following three confessional points:

1. Reformed Christianity is a species of historic Christianity. As such, it confesses its faith in the triune God who created the heav-

ens and the earth and whose second person became incarnate in Jesus of Nazareth.

2. Reformed Christianity holds the Bible to be the prime authority for faith and life, inspired by God and infallible with respect to its purpose. The Bible reveals the identity and work of the triune God in telling the story of creation, the fall of humankind, the covenant established between God and a chosen people, the redemption of many peoples from all nations by the sacrificial work of the promised Messiah, and the reconciliation of all things through the power of the Spirit.

3. Reformed Christianity is part of the one, holy, catholic, and apostolic Church. It adopts a presbyterian form of government and is marked by the preaching of the Word of God, the administration of the sacraments, and firm church discipline.

These three tenets testify to both the ecumenical and the particular moments of Reformed identity. Beyond the creeds which all Christian communions accept, different families of Calvinism staked out their positions in confessions that differentiated their adherents from Roman Catholic and other Protestant Christians. In the species of Calvinism which flowered in the Low Countries during the sixteenth and seventeenth centuries, the confessions which express the Patristic, Protestant, and particularly Reformed consensus are the Belgic Confession, the Heidelberg Catechism, and the Canons of Dort.

In the two centuries following the sixteenth, Calvinism witnessed an attempt by theologians to articulate ever more clearly what it is that Calvinists believe. This period of shoring up Reformed identity by producing large works of theological erudition is known as the period of Protestant Orthodoxy. Such doctrinal Calvinism seemed ill-prepared, however, to meet the broad and sweeping challenges of the Enlightenment. As Christendom stood either powerless or mesmerized in the face of increasing threats to its very existence — the modern scientific worldview, the recourse to human reason as the final arbiter in matters of belief, the emergent historical-critical investigation of the Bible — Protestantism was busy forging a variety of responses: digging in, the approach taken by orthodoxy; opting out, the maneuver favored by pietism; and making deals, the strategy recommended by liberalism.

Another kind of response to the secularizing influence of the Enlightenment and its political embodiment in the French Revolution was conceived by certain Protestants in the Netherlands. In an attempt to re-establish order on the continent after the Napoleonic wars, King William I reorganized the Dutch Reformed Church *(Nederlandse Hervormde Kerk)* as a unified state church in 1816 — a move which brought about a secession *(Afscheiding)* from the DRC in 1834 by pious and doctrinally concerned members of that church. Some of these seceders left for America in the 1840s and settled in West Michigan. In the Netherlands, meanwhile, Groen van Prinsterer (1801-76) and his theological descendants, most notably Abraham Kuyper (1837-1920), were busy articulating a critique of what they took to be an idolatrous revolutionary spirit in Europe.

Trained as a liberal theologian, Kuyper experienced a conversion in his first pastorate through which he came to see the full power of the Calvinism he had too glibly passed over in his youth. Afterward, in addition to the strictly theological work he undertook with his colleague Herman Bavinck (1854-1921), he committed himself to the translation of Calvinism into a political and cultural program that was to renew Dutch society according to Christian principles. While fully cognizant of the reality of common grace operating in the world at large, Kuyper nonetheless proposed an isomorphic plan of Reformed Christian witness in Dutch society: if there was a press, then there would be a Christian press; if a labor union, then a Christian labor union; if a political party, then a Christian political party; if day schools, then Christian day schools; if a university, then a Christian university. Kuyper's accomplishments in realizing much of this point-for-point program of renewal were prodigious, both in terms of what he himself achieved in the Netherlands and how his principles were applied by subsequent generations, including those who came to shape the mission of Calvin College.

The origins of Calvin College lie in the literary department of a Grand Rapids theological school founded in the year 1876. The nineteenth-century Dutch immigrants who had left the Dutch Reformed Church in the Netherlands soon left the Reformed Church in America as well, establishing in 1857 the True Dutch Reformed Church, later known as the Christian Reformed Church. By founding their own theological school some nineteen years later, they were attempting first and foremost to fill the pulpits of their churches with ministers committed to and trained in orthodox Christianity as they understood it. Their concern at the time was the survival and purity of their small community of faith in a foreign land, not the comprehensive transformation of North American society and culture.

But the educational needs of the supporting community soon expanded beyond the preparation of the pastorate. Teachers for Christian day schools of the Dutch Reformed community had to be trained as well. At the end of the century a college was organized around the school's literary department so that, in the words of Synod, "our young people . . . no longer have to wander in various institutions outside our circles, but can be molded by our own Reformed interests" (*Acts of Synod,* 1898, p. 57). John Calvin Junior College, as it was then known, broadened its program to instruct aspiring teachers in a wide range of subjects. The curriculum evolved, reaching into the classical tradition of liberal arts education even as it extended into domains of modern science. The college granted its first Bachelor of Arts degree as a four-year institution in 1921. After the Second World War, its student population exploded. In the 1960s it moved to a new and expansive campus on the edge of town, adopted a discipline-based curriculum and department structure modeled largely on the plan of the research university, and added several professional programs. Among its faculty, mostly Calvin alumni, were many who had received advanced degrees from some of the most prestigious graduate schools on the North American continent.

With such growth and accomplishment came a new sense of cultural confidence that found its proper expression in the Kuyperian worldview. No longer did Calvin conceive of its purpose as shielding students from the secular influence of American society; rather, it was to prepare and send them into that society as agents of transformation. No longer a mere refuge for orthodoxy, it became a training ground for cultural engagement. Now with a student population of some 4,000, 250 faculty members, major concentrations in over seventy areas, eight professional programs, and 46,000 alumni, Calvin College has emerged from its sheltered and provincial existence and entered the mainstream of North American higher education with a solid reputation for academic excellence and its Reformed voice still strong and clear. The ecclesiastical conflicts that originally defined the Reformation have now faded into the historical background. The Enlightenment project that first elicited the Kuyperian response is largely exhausted. The College now steps into a postmodern world, and is once again called upon to embody an education that is academically rigorous, culturally relevant, deeply Christian, and thoroughly Reformed.

The Theological Strand

The word "Reformed" describes the Protestant churches rooted in the Swiss Reformation and organized on the basis of a presbyterian form of government. In that sense, it is an ecclesiastical term. But it has a distinct theological sense as well.

Rooted in the Reformation's insistence on the sole authority of scripture for true knowledge of God, the Reformed theological tradition sought to forge doctrines that would serve as a faithful and consistent expression of its primary source. Educated in the humanist tradition of literary scholarship, John Calvin recognized the signal importance of rigorous training in the liberal arts and a thorough knowledge of the Patristic tradition for the conduct of theology. For these are an invaluable help in rendering the content of scripture accurately, and presenting it persuasively. For this reason Calvin and his theological descendants did not make an enemy of reason and tradition in their attempt to elevate the faith. Rather, they sought to make allies of them according to a certain agreement as to their roles and mutual relationships: the authority of scripture above the authority of tradition, whose role was to develop and retain right interpretation of scripture; faith serving as a guide to reason, whose primary task was to make the content of faith both perspicuous and persuasive.

In terms of the sources of theology, then, Reformed theology draws on the following in descending order of authority: scripture; the traditions of the church; reason and experience. With respect to the first two sources, Reformed theology recognizes the importance of fidelity to the Christian scriptures and fealty to the Christian tradition of which it is the custodian. Theology must therefore be biblical and confessional. With respect to the third source, Reformed theology recognizes the importance of continued reflection and dynamic engagement with contemporary culture. Theology must also be dialogical.

This ordering of sources has direct implications for theological method. Reformed theology seeks to draw on the Bible as interpreted by the tradition in order to speak a word in the present that is faithful, relevant, and coherent. Reformed theology is therefore an ongoing activity, never finished, running between past and present, in each generation seeking anew to make sense of the faith passed down to it in the time in which it lives. The spirit of the theological project thus understood is captured in the Reformed slogan *ecclesia reformata semper reformanda est:* a reformed church is always to be reforming. In so thinking of the theological task, the Reformed tradition was repeating in its own words an old and venerable way of posing the relation between faith and reason. St. Augustine and St. Anselm conceived of that relationship along the lines of the famous dictum *fides quaerens intellectum:* faith seeking understanding. As in the slogan of the Reformation, there is something stable (faith — an enduring foundation) and yet something dynamic (the search for understanding — a restless quest).

In its theological emphases beyond the ecumenical teachings regarding the nature of God and Christ, the Reformed tradition — taking its cues from the opening and closing acts of scripture, the first article of the Apostles' Creed, and Book One of Calvin's *Institutes* — has sought to make foundational sense of the belief in God the Father who out of nothing created the heavens and the earth. In other words, the Reformed tradition has taken the doctrine of creation to be central to a well-formed theological understanding of the world and the calling of the Christian within it. The doctrine of creation forms the steady and ultimate context for understanding the tragic meaning of humanity's fall into sin, the scope of salvation through the atoning work of Christ, the restoration of all things through the power of the Spirit, and the arena of service that we render to God out of gratitude for electing us as recipients of his grace. Reformed Christians believe that because all things find their ultimate source in God, creation and all of human life within its boundaries, fallen as they may be, remain capable of redirection and worthy of redemption. Despite the rebellion of the human race, God has continued to provide for creation, promised to redeem it, and sent his only-begotten Son, who took upon himself full humanity in order to accomplish that redemption.

World-flight, cultural disengagement, and Gnostic escape theories of redemption have therefore never been hallmarks of a Reformed Christianity that understands the bracing implications of its own theology. By its lights, the Christian life cannot be an inward piety cut off from all worldly involvement, nor can it be divided into a program of social action without remainder. Reformed spirituality insists on the wedding of personal piety and cultural engagement, where each complements and energizes the other in the response of the whole person to the call of God. In Reformed circles there have been countless lives of Christian vocation spent in business enterprises, scientific endeavors, public service, cultural activity, the helping professions, and educational institutions in addition to those called to serve the institutional church. Such devotion to the welfare of a fallen but good creation, worked out in manifold vocations, has been the mark and mainspring of Reformed people at their best, the cultural expression of a "holy worldliness" to which they have been called.

Appendix III

The Practical Strand

The practical implications of Reformed Christianity — under the aegis of a robust doctrine of creation — are wide-ranging indeed. Some of these implications have been indicated in the previous section on the theological nature of the tradition. With the twin notions of the sovereignty of God and the integrity of creation, Reformed Christians have understood themselves to be charged with a task in this earthly life, a cultural mandate: be busy doing the Father's work in this world; tend the garden; rule it wisely; develop, explore, and care for it in anticipation of its deliverance from suffering made possible by the Son through the life-giving Spirit.

The Reformed emphasis on world-engagement should be understood in the historical context of the Reformation. Many of the doctors of the church had been thoroughly schooled in the ways of Greek philosophy. And so they imbibed much of the worldview of the Greek philosophers. Many of them thought of the human soul as defined by its powers of knowing, and therefore thought of the fulfillment of human life as an intellectual matter. The intellect finds its completion in knowledge of the highest possible object of knowledge — namely, God. In the afterlife, the saved will be admitted to this exalted form of cognition, called the "beatific vision." In this life they could only anticipate it with fleeting glimpses of the divine essence achieved through prayer and meditation. Those who were serious about the religious life would leave their occupations in this world and retreat to the monasteries, where the daily schedule was organized around the demands of divine contemplation.

Luther was a monk before he was a reformer. When he broke with the church over the theology of justification, he also broke with the contemplative ideal of the religious life. We are to love our neighbors, Luther taught, not leave them in pursuit of our own spiritual fulfillment. God calls us not to abandon our worldly occupations, but to serve our neighbors through them. This is the Christian's calling. And Calvin agreed. Those who recommend the contemplative life, he wrote in his commentary on Mark 10, appear to be "indebted to Aristotle, who places the highest good, and ultimate end, of human life in contemplation." On the contrary, Calvin claims, we know we were created for the express purpose of being employed in labor of various kinds, and that no sacrifice is more pleasing to God than when we apply ourselves diligently to our own callings, and endeavor to live in such a way as to contribute to the common good.

In the Reformed tradition, then, a high view of creation translates into a high view of culture and the engaged life. Reformed Christians take it as their vocation to exercise their gifts and abilities in a life of service to the human community. But they also realize that the conditions under which they do so are less than pristine. For God's good creation has been twisted by the corrupting power of human sin and disobedience, introducing a deep spiritual division in humanity as people turn to or away from God's offer of salvation in Christ. Faithful cultural engagement will involve not only the development of creation's many potentials, but a struggle against the evil and falsehood that insinuate themselves in every area of human life, indeed, in every human soul; it will be a contest of opposing principles that runs the entire width and breadth of creation.

Kuyper called the Reformed theological understanding of creation that served as a basis for such broad cultural engagement a Christian "world-and-life view" *(wereld- en levensbeschouwing)*, adapting a term of common use in nineteenth-century German scholarship *(Weltanschauung)*. In recognition of the universal lordship of Jesus Christ, Kuyper was eager to break down the Enlightenment tendency to privatize and marginalize the Christian faith, to box it into the corner of personal piety. In using the term "worldview" and its variants, he was concerned to communicate his conviction that Christian principles should inform the totality of our being and doing, not just our theology, personal conduct, and church life. The lordship of Jesus Christ is universal, he maintained, extending over every square inch of our world.

A liberal arts college that not only roots itself in the Reformed Christian tradition, but consistently derives its sense of mission from its theology, will construe its task as a divine calling to broad-based

189

participation in the life of the academic disciplines and the conscientious preparation of its students to pursue their callings in professions, cultural domains, and societal spheres that extend far beyond its walls. Working out the calling of the college will involve the creation of an academic community that is ordered by the rule of Christian life and informed by the hope of the gospel, a disciplined pursuit of knowledge in service of the Christian church and the human community at large, a steady commitment to tracing out the implications of the faith for the entire encyclopedia of knowledge, and the fitting of students with the knowledge, skills, and dispositions they will need if they are to take on the cultural tasks of the communities they are destined to serve.

But even that is not quite enough. To do justice to the full scope of Reformed Christian faith and practice, such a college must emphasize not only its cultural mandate in God's good creation but also the significance of the mission mandate in a fallen world. Its engagement with culture must be stamped by the good news of the gospel of Jesus Christ. It must help its students learn how to tell the Christian story, live in Christian expectation, wage Christian critique, offer hope and healing in Christ's name to the downtrodden, the outcast, and all those whose lives have been damaged by the sway of sin, and so point to the triune God in whose image all human beings are created and in whose offer of redemption humanity may share. By recognizing the propriety of the mission mandate in a fallen world, the college and the community it serves remind themselves of the tragic depth of human sin and the height of God's redemptive love in Christ, and thus protect themselves against the danger of losing their Christian identity within the mundane commitments to cultural involvement.

What, then, does it mean to be Reformed? The Reformed community strives after the lofty goal of retaining and representing the best of the Christian tradition, replete with orthodox and coherent doctrines of the Trinity and Christ, a vibrant conception of the authority of scripture in matters of faith and life, a high doctrine of creation, an honest estimation of the depth and scope of human sin, a broad view of redemption, and a deep appreciation of the value of everyday life as a field of mutual service in response to a divine vocation. To be Reformed at Calvin College is to preserve, extend, and publish this interpretation of the Christian faith, to engage in the rigors and the rewards of the academic life as a Christian calling, and to prepare students for their respective vocations, ever mindful of the aching distance between the basic goodness of this fallen world for which God incarnate died and the surpassing splendor of the world which is to come and for which all Christians hope.

The Ideal of Liberal Arts Education

The description of the core requirements in Calvin's catalog appear under the heading "The Liberal Arts Core." Behind this brief title stands the long and complex history of liberal arts education, a history that begins in the classical period of Western civilization, courses through the schools of the Middle Ages, and intertwines with the Reformed tradition in ways both intimate and, for our purposes, instructive.

Although the phrase *"artes liberales"* is first recorded in the writings of Cicero, the Roman orator, the tradition of liberal arts education has its origins in the emergence of democracy in ancient Athens. In a heady political culture no longer based on the fiat of a king of the will of the oligarchs, the public fortunes of the citizens of Athens were largely dictated by their powers of persuasive speech in the *agora*. Thus a market for instruction in the art of spoken rhetoric was created — and soon filled by such itinerant teachers as Hippias, Protagoras and Gorgias. Known as the sophists, they were vilified in the Platonic dialogues for their willingness to equip their students with the skills of speech without regard for truth or ethical principle. In reaction to these vendors of words in the markets of power, Plato proposed to mobilize human speech in the interests of philosophical dialectic, which was not designed to manipulate the opinions of the masses for personal advantage, but to transcend the domain of opinion altogether in the direction of a genuine knowledge of the Good —

a knowledge which would in turn serve as the moral foundation for the restoration of an Athens deeply troubled after its defeat in the Peloponnesian Wars. Plato's invitation to such critical sifting of received opinion under the watchful eye of reason, however, led to apparently endless disputation and a wholesale lack of stable results. The goal of sure knowledge — not to mention the application of such knowledge to politics — soon receded to infinity.

Between the quick pragmatic grasp for political power by the sophists and the endless pursuit of rationally grounded knowledge by the philosophers, a third option was marked out by Isocrates, a contemporary of Plato: the wedding of rhetorical skill to traditional wisdom. In his work, *Against the Sophists,* he faulted the sophists for their lack of moral principles; but in the *Antidosis* he also criticized the philosophers for their ineffectual abstractions. The true orator must be good — and effective. Students of Isocrates were shaped in character according to the wisdom of the age through exposure to canonical texts in the study of grammar. They were then taught to make that wisdom eloquent and persuasive through training in the art of rhetoric. Dialectic, as the method for discovering truth and testing opinion, played a subordinate role in their education.

The option of Isocrates was carried into the Roman world by Cicero and Quintilian, whose manuals on rhetoric became the founding texts of the liberal arts tradition in the West. That tradition, however, was soon destined to be transformed. With the collapse of the Roman Empire and the disappearance of republican forms of governance, there was little need for the art of rhetoric as a tool of civic discourse. But with the rise of Christianity, liberal arts education was soon employed in the service of other goals. The clash between pagan classical culture and Christianity in the patristic period was reconciled by St. Augustine, himself an accomplished teacher of rhetoric prior to his dramatic conversion. Training in grammar, logic, and rhetoric was both good and necessary, Augustine held, for understanding the truth embedded in an authoritative scripture and assisting in the soul's ascent to a knowledge of God. Thus were the liberal arts made to serve the needs of biblical interpretation, the elaboration of Christian theology, and the private life of piety. They were eventually codified in the Middle Ages into seven subjects — the *trivium* (grammar, rhetoric, and logic), and the *quadrivium* (arithmetic, geometry, music, and astronomy). With the development of the great European universities in the twelfth century, the liberal arts were tied to broader social aims as preparation for more specialized studies in the faculties of law, medicine, and theology.

With the rise of the schools, however, also came the ascendence of scholasticism. The introduction of the philosophical texts of Aristotle into Europe during the twelfth century occasioned a new synthesis in the thirteenth of pagan philosophy and Christianity by leading lights of the Dominican order, most notably Albert the Great and Thomas Aquinas. As this synthesis established itself at the University of Paris and elsewhere, the curriculum leading to the study of theology was reorganized. Among the liberal arts, logic was given precedence over rhetoric, and the role of character formation in the study of grammar was de-emphasized. The liberal arts as a whole were preparatory to the study of philosophy, which was divided according to the broad Aristotelian distinctions between nature, morality, and metaphysics. Philosophy was in turn preparatory to the study of theology. And theology itself shifted from the symbolic biblical theology of the earlier centuries to a dialectical theology which aimed to convert the tenets of the Christian faith into a comprehensive system of propositions based on the plan of Aristotelian categories and distinctions. This new program in the schools came to be known as the *via antiqua,* and it unleashed a period of intense philosophical activity that eventually degenerated into overly subtle disputation with little connection to the life of Christian piety or the needs of the church and the world.

The scholastic subordination of rhetoric to logic and the orientation of liberal arts as a whole to the philosophical project of speculative knowledge soon elicited a strong reaction in the form of Renaissance humanism. The humanists of the fourteenth and fifteenth centuries drew upon the old Roman civic ideal of liberal arts education, the rhetorical tradition of literary study geared to the demands of the active life and the development of the human personality. This grand movement, tied to the flourishing of civic culture in northern Italy and spurred by the re-discovery of the full texts of Quintilian's *Institutio Oratoria* in 1416 and Cicero's *De Oratore* in 1422, gave birth to a program of study known as the *studia humanitatis*. The schools of northern Italy became the center for this reinvention of liberal education, a new course of study that soon spread to the secular courts, urban centers, and eventually to the universities of Europe and England, finding its most striking advocate in the celebrated figure of Erasmus (1469-1536), the "Colossus of Rotterdam."

In the culture wars that ensued between the scholastics and humanists, the Protestant reformers without exception took the side of the humanists, recommending an education aimed at the cultivation of the language arts and the promotion of true piety. They had, after all, just elevated the authority of the biblical text over that of the institutional church. They saw in the humanist program of study the literary tools they needed to recover the teachings of the Bible, which were to provide leverage over an ecclesiastical tradition they were convinced had gone astray. In addition, humanities helped make the preaching and teaching of the fresh message of scripture persuasive among the people and the courts of Europe. In the Lutheran camp, Melanchthon reasserted the priority of rhetoric over logic in the arts curriculum of Wittenberg. Calvin, trained as a humanist scholar in France, modeled the college at Geneva on the school in Strasbourg organized by Johannes Sturm, where a simple faith was to be combined with classical learning in order to produce a "wise and eloquent piety." From Geneva this approach to liberal arts education spread throughout the Reformed countries on the continent, and to England through the work of John Colet and Roger Ascham. In New England, the colonial colleges were modeled on the colleges of Oxford and Cambridge, where they first drew their professorate. Harvard was fashioned after Emmanuel College of Cambridge University, a Puritan stronghold; William and Mary after Queen's College, Oxford.

Thus the colleges of seventeenth- and eighteenth-century America continued the rhetorical tradition of liberal arts education. As centers of instruction according to a classical curriculum, typically tied to a religious tradition, they endeavored to form and prepare their students for lives of civic service in the various professions. The emphasis was on teaching, the cultivation of aptitudes and character by moral guidance and by literary induction into the stream of canonical culture. Moreover, teaching was conducted on the regency rather than the professorial system: typically, one teacher would instruct an entire class of students in all subjects throughout their four-year stay. In many instances, the president of the college taught a capstone course in "moral philosophy" to all seniors, a course that was integrative and, in today's terms, interdisciplinary. The curriculum was the same for all — one big core — with no electives and no majors. In Europe, as in the States, open-ended research was conducted largely outside the sphere of both the college and university. The development of the new experimental sciences of nature took place in learned societies; philosophers, for the most part, moved among the landed aristocracy.

This arrangement, however, was to change dramatically with the cultural ascendancy of the German research university in the nineteenth century, beginning with the founding of the University of Berlin in 1810 by Wilhelm von Humbolt. Placing the Enlightenment project of free inquiry — the generation of new knowledge untethered by religious dogma and unconnected to practical concerns — at the center of the university enterprise, the German model of higher education created an environment geared to the vigorous pursuit of specialized research and the training of future researchers. The classical curriculum was dismantled and divided according to the separate disciplines; the new disciplines of the natural sciences were brought on board and given equal footing; autonomous departments were created on the basis of this array of disciplines; students could elect majors in specific disciplines. Hiring and promotion policies favored and fostered the research ethos. University faculty lived not to teach so much as to write.

In the course of the nineteenth century the German universities amassed a great deal of prestige — and a good number of American graduate students — on the basis of their impressive advances in research accomplished under their auspices. By comparison, the older and more diffuse form of education at the liberal arts college began to look decidedly second rate, at best preparatory for university-level work.

The German research model entered the American scene with the founding of Johns Hopkins University in 1876. Thomas Huxley delivered the main address at this momentous event. A zealous advocate of the ethos of free inquiry, Huxley argued in his well-known essay, "Science and Culture," that "liberal education" should be founded upon "an unhesitating faith that the free employment of reason, in accordance with scientific method, is the sole method of reaching truth." It is fair to say that the research model took American higher education by storm. Institution after institution fashioned itself after the German university in ethos and infrastructure. The old classical curriculum was broken down into its component disciplines, which in turn became several of the many options students could elect to pursue as major concentrations if they were so inclined. Departments were formed. Research was promoted. Religious ties were loosened. Graduate programs were expanded.

The dramatic change in the complexion of American higher education put the liberal arts colleges in a culturally awkward position. Andrew D. White, the first president of Cornell University, described them in 1865 as a "regime of petty sectarian colleges." William Rainey Harper, president of the University of Chicago, claimed in 1900 that such colleges would soon find their place as advanced preparatory schools for the universities. Three years later, Starr Jordan, president of Stanford University, predicted that "the college will disappear" — the best of the colleges will become universities; the others will become secondary schools.

Jordan's prediction came true, for the most part, with the following modifications. During the first half of the twentieth century, not just the best of the colleges became universities; most of them did. They did so not by adding graduate programs and awarding advanced degrees, but by adopting the curriculum, infrastructure, and ethos of the research universities at their own station. Their curriculum was reorganized according to the separate disciplines; autonomous departments were created; and research was promoted even as the primary commitment to undergraduate teaching was maintained. Many colleges also sought to create an atmosphere of free inquiry, thus starting the engines of secularization, while at the same time maintaining nominal ties to a religious tradition or denomination. Thus most liberal arts colleges in America today are a curious hybrid: they contain the vestigial organs of the old classical curriculum, with its emphasis on teaching and instruction according to a common tradition; but those organs are now surrounded and encased by the newer vital systems of the modern research university, which were designed for specialized, open-ended research.

In the 1960s Calvin College participated in the internal replication of the research university model on the undergraduate level, advocating the "disciplinary view" of liberal arts education. It did not, however, at the same time suggest that inquiry within the disciplines should be loosened from its religious mooring. Far from it. All inquiry was to be conducted from a Christian perspective. But the disciplinary view was designed to make Calvin College safe for research — more like a university in structure, if not in commitment to the ideal of autonomous reason — thus forever changing the focus and feel of the institution. The statement on curriculum in which this view was codified, *Christian Liberal Arts Education,* is still in force today. And it is to this document we now turn.

The Purpose of the Core Curriculum

Today Calvin College is a comprehensive institution of higher learning rooted in the liberal arts tradition. However, since the reorganization of Calvin's curriculum in the late 1960s according to the disciplinary model proposed in CLAE *(Christian Liberal Arts Education)* the purpose of liberal arts education carried in the core curriculum has been less than perfectly clear. There should be little mystery to this. For there are two agendas at work in CLAE. One ties into the classical ideal of liberal arts education as personal formation and preparation for involvement in civic life; the other hooks up with the more narrowly focused ideal of the modern research university, the training of knowledge workers for the fields of academe. In its broad statements of purpose for Christian education, CLAE clearly aligns itself with the former: the aim of Christian education, it claims, "is to train students to live the life of faith in contemporary society" (CLAE, p. 40). Yet, when we come to its specific interpretation of the liberal arts ideal, the emphasis swings in the direction of the disciplinary research agenda. After faulting the classical ideal of liberal education championed by William Harry Jellema for its "passivity," CLAE issues the following injunction: "We must ourselves develop the various disciplines; and . . . we must educate new generations for productive and creative work in the various disciplines" (CLAE, p. 46). A page later CLAE repeats the point, asserting that, "The primary focus of a Christian liberal arts education should be on teachers and students together engaging in the various scholarly disciplines" (CLAE, p. 47). The aims of the general education program at Calvin — later called the "Core Curriculum" — are then spelled out exclusively in terms of the separate disciplines and never move beyond their scope. Through a set of distribution requirements, students are to become acquainted with the *results* of the disciplines, the *methods* of the disciplines, and the variety of *approaches* within the disciplines (CLAE, pp. 61-62). While there is some speculation in CLAE as to how the disinterested study of the disciplines will prepare students to live the Christian life in contemporary society — say, through the acquisition of generic intellectual skills (CLAE, pp. 63-67) — the connection between the two remains tenuous, vague, and unconvincing. The one interdisciplinary course that was to serve as the flagship of integrative common learning in the new curriculum — Christian Perspectives on Learning — was no sooner proposed than it was converted into a distribution option in the contextual disciplines. The "Core Curriculum" was implemented minus its core.

The Ultimate Purpose of the Core Curriculum

Thus there emerges within CLAE a gap between the ultimate goal of Christian liberal arts education as preparing students for a life of service in contemporary society, and the proximate aim of general education as introducing students to the disinterested study of the disciplines (as if they were being prepared for a life of service in contemporary academia). We propose a stronger link, a more direct connection, between the ultimate goal of Christian education and the core curriculum by suggesting that the primary aim of core courses in the disciplines should not be a general introduction to the disciplines, but an introduction — from the vantage points of the disciplines — to the world in which our students are called to serve, taught in ways that foster both the commitment and the ability to serve. The *Expanded Statement of Mission* puts the point this way: because "we are called to obey God as whole persons in every area of life, . . . education should explicitly connect the way we think with the way we live" (ESM, p. 18). The chief aim of core courses in history, then, is not to present the discipline of history — its results, methods, and approaches — but to present the world in which students are called to participate as historical agents, to examine the formation of those ideas, themes, institutions, and practices that have shaped both their identities and the society they inhabit, to kindle a passion for the purposes of God in human culture, and to cultivate the habits of mind they must possess if they are to make good on that passion. Likewise, core courses in political science should not be designed as general introductions to the discipline of political science, but to the major political ideas, institutions, practices, issues, and tensions that students will grapple with as committed Christian citizens. Similar points could be made with respect to every discipline represented in the core.

It might seem that this proposal is more a matter of semantics than substance. The disciplines, after all, study the world, not themselves. To involve students in the study of the disciplines is thus already to involve them in the study of the world. We grant this point but still maintain that the disciplines can be engaged with different

199

purposes in mind, and that a difference in purpose will make a difference in instruction. The line drawn from audience to objective will intersect the disciplines at different angles as audience and objective vary: if we are teaching our core courses to prospective majors with the intent of introducing them to our discipline, we will write the syllabus one way; if we are teaching students who will probably not pursue our discipline with the intent of providing them what they need for informed engagement in that aspect of life we trade in, then we will write the syllabus another way. If a core course in philosophy were simply an introduction to the discipline, then almost any topic that has engaged the minds of philosophers could go into the mix. If it weren't for the antecedent limitations of student interest and ability, a semester's introductory course in philosophy could be composed of causal theories of linguistic reference, the modal problem of transworld identity, early modern theories of perceptual consciousness, and the fine points of Leibniz's monadology. But if the course were designed to help students identify and deal with the philosophical issues embedded in life as it now confronts us, it would more likely devote itself to such problems as moral and cognitive relativism, the relation between scientific theory and religious belief, the claims to truth in a self-consciously pluralistic society, the phenomena of certainty and doubt in the domain of faith, the evolutionary explanation of human behavior, sexual ethics, and the like. (It should go without saying that such a course, in being directed to contemporary issues, need not limit itself to contemporary texts. Some of the best resources for gaining perspectives on these issues may be found in texts that come to us from other ages and other cultures.)

The chief questions, then, to be asked in shaping the content of the core curriculum are these: what are the basic domains of the practical world in which we live out our various callings; and what must we know, become, and be able to do if we are to pursue our callings in these domains effectively? The disciplines will surely have a great deal to contribute here, not by calling attention to themselves, but by directing a focused look at that aspect of the world they know best. As the *Expanded Statement of Mission* puts it: "The classroom is a context for looking outward, for equipping students with an understanding of the world in which they live and for bringing a redemptive message to that world" (ESM, p. 25). Core courses should be taught not as if they were the first course students might take in a major, but the last one they take before they find their places in the world beyond Calvin's campus. They should serve as windows on the world, not the academy.

Such, we submit, is the purpose of the core curriculum as it relates to the overarching goal of a Calvin education, the goal of enabling Christians to live effectively in contemporary society. A major concentration or professional program should enable our students to live a life of Christian service in their chosen professions. The core should enable them to do so in the other and equally important domains of their calling — the family, the church, the nation, the marketplace, the various venues of the arts, and the like. It should provide them with a basic understanding of the history, structure, themes, issues, and interaction within and among these various realms of practical life. It should furnish them with biblically informed insights so that they may enter these realms as ambassadors of Christ, well equipped to represent and advance the redemptive purposes of God's kingdom. Insofar as this education looks beyond the walls of the academy, beyond the "methods, results, and approaches" of the various disciplines, its focus is "external" — it prepares students to respond to their vocations in the broad, rich, and Reformed sense of that term.

The Proximate Purposes of the Core Curriculum

To capture the connection between the core curriculum and the overarching educational mission of the college is to set before us a goal that lies far beyond four years of education at Calvin. But if the core is to serve that ultimate goal well, it must also perform certain crucial functions during those four years. For a well-designed core curriculum should further a number of structural purposes internal to a college program of study, lest it become nothing more than a loose and

201

ungainly collection of disciplinary offerings bound only by the criterion of practical relevance. In addition to preparing students for a life of effective service, the core curriculum should help found, integrate, unify, order, and mark a Calvin education.

The proximate purposes of the core curriculum at Calvin College, then, are the following:

1. It should assure that certain proficiencies are in place in the early stages of academic work at Calvin, so that students are well prepared to make progress in their subsequent studies. In this sense, the core curriculum will be *foundational*.
2. It should establish integrative frameworks for study at Calvin, so that the particular forms of knowledge acquired in the disciplines connect, mutually reinforce, and illuminate each other. In this sense, the core curriculum will be *contextual*.
3. It should provide a common fund of intellectual experience, a common vocabulary for cross-disciplinary discussion, and thus create the conditions for an academic community that extends beyond the purview of the department, the major, or the program. In this sense, the core curriculum will be *central*.
4. It should provide intelligent sequencing in the order of core studies, so that important common themes and skills get developed throughout the four years of a Calvin education, with core courses building on each other according to students' level of expertise and intellectual maturity. In this sense, the core curriculum will be *continual*.
5. It should convey Calvin's Reformed identity, so that students, whatever their major or program, will have a significant exposure to a Reformed Christian understanding of reality and their place within it, acquiring a sense for how their work in the world could count as a response to God's call to serve in his kingdom. In this sense, the core curriculum will be *confessional*.

Thus the questions of basic college proficiencies, contextualization, commonality, sequence, and confessional identity should be taken into account as chief desiderata in reviewing and revising the present core curriculum at Calvin. In most cases, these proximate purposes will not call for additional content in the core; rather, they will lend focus, definition, and a limit to its structure. They demand that decisions be made about what belongs to a true core of common courses and what belongs to the distribution requirements; what comes first in the order of study and what comes later; what should appear as a thematic component of many core courses and what should be consolidated in a single core course; and the like.

Whatever the particulars of these decisions turn out to be, the resulting structure of the core curriculum will most likely resemble a column rather than a simple foundation. To date, the core has been a series of distribution requirements that students "get out of the way" in the first two years of their academic work at Calvin. It serves as a kind of platform from which they launch their programs or major concentrations, leaving it far behind, a rapidly diminishing image in the rearview mirror of their career rocket. But if the core is to serve its purposes — both ultimate and proximate — as envisioned in this statement, it must become more like a column that rises up through the center of a Calvin education, providing central structural support at each level, as it is implemented in common learning courses, object-oriented distribution requirements, and the educational programming of the student life division, and as its goals are deepened in the major concentration or professional program.

Since the adoption of CLAE, Calvin has been steadily fashioning itself after the image of the research university (*cum* professional school, since PECLAC). It should come as no surprise, then, that the college is now dealing with many of the educational problems that currently beset the larger universities: hyper-specialization, curricular fragmentation, departmental empire building, a lack of cross-disciplinary conversation, and, to some degree, the loss of academic community. The tension between the ideals of the liberal arts college and those of the research university that Calvin now experiences is, nonetheless, one that we should cheerfully, if carefully, embrace. For there are many things on both sides of the divide that deserve our wholehearted support: on the one hand, the commitment to serious participation in the life of the disciplines, the promotion of cutting-edge scholarship and Reformed witness in the professional guilds, and all the benefits that active research brings to the classroom by way of expertise and excitement; on the other hand, the commitment to a well-rounded and contextual education, the attention to the holistic formation of students, and their preparation for a broad-based engagement of life that is guided by Christian commitment.

Nevertheless, in recent years the balance of the curriculum and organization of the college has tipped in the direction of the research ethos, with all the attendant problems mentioned above. However necessary CLAE was in its time, however appropriate it was to establish the disciplines, to make room for research, and to lend autonomy to the departments, it is now incumbent upon us to devote serious thought to the status of liberal arts education as it is carried out in the core curriculum, to make it more than a sampling of various academic disciplines, so that we can say with integrity that this part of the college — its core — has both engaged the world and prepared students for a life of effective Christian service within it.

In the following three sections, we divide the content of the core curriculum into the broad areas of knowledge, skills, and virtues. Under these headings we have given specific statements of the curricular and pedagogical objectives of the core. These statements flesh out in some detail what we have in mind when we speak of the ultimate purposes of the core; and they provide the raw material that will be required if the core is to fulfill its proximate purposes as well. Some forms of knowledge are directly relevant to informed participation in the domains of practical life, some will also serve as integrative frameworks for college study; some skills listed are required for a life of effective service in society, some must also be in place as basic proficiencies for college-level work; all of the virtues will do double duty, serving to build academic community and to shape character for a life of Christian discipleship in the world at large. The final decision on the place, weight, and role of these elements in the core curriculum is worked out in the Proposal for the Core Curriculum.

Core Knowledge

The Expanded Statement of Mission organizes its comments on the content to be conveyed in the core curriculum under the broadly Augustinian headings of knowing God, knowing the world, and knowing ourselves. Here we follow that arrangement, and articulate under subheadings those specific forms of knowledge we wish to extend to all Calvin students. Please note: This is a list of topics to be covered in the core curriculum, not a list of core courses; moreover, it should not be assumed that each topic entry carries equal weight.

Knowledge of God

"At the heart of our programs lies the pursuit of knowledge of our triune God as revealed in scripture and creation, and as expressed through religious traditions in general and the Reformed Christian tradition in particular."

An Expanded Statement
of the Mission of Calvin College

I. The Christian Faith

Calvin College is a Christian college. Its students should acquire in the core curriculum a mature and reflective knowledge of the triune

God as revealed in the Bible and interpreted by the Christian tradition. They should develop a deeper understanding of the works and ways of God as disclosed in the biblical canon and presented in the great themes of creation, fall, redemption, and restoration of all things in Christ; as summarized in the ecumenical creeds; and as systematized in the discipline of theology. They should acquire an awareness of the global dimensions of the Christian religion, its vital and diverse cultural expressions, its movement through time and across the continents. Moreover, their own reading of holy scripture should be well acquainted with the issues of biblical interpretation, their theological understandings tested in the intellectual climate of our day, so that they may responsibly articulate the central beliefs of the Christian faith to themselves and to others in this secular age, ready to serve as informed members and leaders of the Christian church.

II. The Reformed Tradition

Calvin College is a Reformed Christian college. Its core curriculum should serve as a primary carrier and passionate advocate of the Reformed interpretation of the Christian faith, making that interpretation compelling and engaging, inviting students to take on and grow into its holistic understanding of the biblical themes of creation, fall, redemption, and restoration; its sense of the radical fallenness and the deep spiritual conflict that play themselves out in all domains of human culture; its insistence that God's sovereignty be honored in every area of human endeavor. Furthermore, in the core curriculum, Calvin's students should become thoroughly acquainted with the salient features of the Reformed tradition: its history and its heroes; its central texts; its cultural impulses; its relation to other communions within the Christian tradition; its strengths and its weaknesses; and, finally, its expression in the Kuyperian tradition, which has, more than any other, served as a primary source in the formation of Calvin's present educational ethos. In possession of such knowledge, its

graduates should find themselves equipped with a deepened understanding of what it means to follow Christ and his way of redemption
in their respective callings. Calvin graduates who enter churches of
the Reformed communion should also find themselves well prepared
to serve as informed parishioners in positions of leadership; those
who enter other communions should have nonetheless an appreciation of the Reformed contribution to the church universal.

III. Other Religious Traditions

Calvin College prepares its graduates to pursue lives of Christian service in the contemporary world. This world contains other major religious traditions that inform the beliefs, practices, institutions, and
cultures of many nations and billions of people. A distinctive feature
of the Reformed tradition is the insight that religions are not the simple creation of human wishes, or mere reflections of dominant social
relations; rather, they are an expression of the *"sensus divinitatis"* that
God, in his common grace, has implanted in all his image bearers.
Calvin students should be familiar with the basic tenets of other
world religions as responses to God's self-disclosure in nature and in
conscience, with the ways of life that they encourage, and with the
points of contact they bear to Christianity. Students should be enabled and encouraged to evaluate the claims of these traditions in the
light of God's revelation in the person of Jesus Christ, interact with
members of these traditions with increased understanding, bear witness to the Christian faith effectively, and acquire deeper insight into
the religious movements that have shaped and continue to shape the
world in which they are called to live out the hope of the gospel.

Knowledge of the World

*Along with the knowledge of God comes "an understanding of God's
world and critical inquiry into its problems and potential. We need to*

understand the structure and integrity of nature, discern the cultural and social forces that shape our world, and address the needs and issues of contemporary life."

*An Expanded Statement
of the Mission of Calvin College*

IV. World Structure

At the core of the religions, philosophies, and ideologies of our age lie intuitions about the basic structure of the world and the purpose of human life within it. Whether reality is exhausted in the material world; whether the material world is but an appearance of a deeper and more lasting reality; whether reality is only a show of appearances in the mind, or, as Calvin put it, the "theater of God's glory"; whether human beings are just complicated animals governed by the principles of pleasure and pain; whether they possess a special faculty that connects them to a rational order that should guide their action; whether they are created in the image of a personal God they are called to know, love, and serve; whether human life ends with physical death or finds its ultimate destiny beyond; whether our sense of right and wrong has any grounds beyond our desires and social conventions; whether history is the sad tale of decline from a golden age, or the heartening story of steady progress; whether evil is a natural part of human life, a passing inconvenience that can be eliminated with the right social program, or the intrusion of an abnormal state of affairs that only God can rectify; whether human reason has the innate power to decide all matters of truth, or stands in need of guidance and correction — such questions get sorted out in a basic view of the world and the purpose of our life within it, in a "world-and-life view." While Calvin students should be encouraged in the life of Christian piety and instructed in the doctrines of the Christian church as interpreted by the Reformed tradition, they should also come to see and appreciate how Christianity opens out to a comprehensive view of the world and human life — how Christian belief translates into a world-

and-life view. They should, moreover, gain a sense for how this view stacks up against its main competitors and alternatives in the marketplace of ideas. In their examination of the issues in the basic domains of practical life, they should learn to trace out the implications of a Christian world-and-life view — how it bears on an understanding of such issues as work and leisure, friendship and sexuality, technology, cultural diversity, education, and politics.

V. Formal and Quantitative Structures

We inhabit a world rich in elegant and intricate formal structures. We move, moreover, in a civilization where the sciences of these structures have become a major cultural force. Much more than a narrow set of computational procedures and techniques, the mathematical disciplines have both opened up a significant aspect of our world and indelibly shaped it. Students at Calvin College should acquire an understanding of the range and basic types of formal and quantitative structures used in the representation of reality, and a generous perspective on their allied disciplines — their history, influence, the nature of their objects, their many fields of endeavor, and their manifold contemporary applications in such diverse areas as empirical research methods and public policy.

VI. The Natural World

The natural world in its many dimensions forms the context and condition of existence we share with all fellow creatures — be they rocks, trees, animals, or fellow human beings. The sciences of the natural world have played a role in Western culture the magnitude of which is difficult to overestimate: they have irrevocably shaped our understanding of ourselves and the world we inhabit; they have brought us deeper knowledge and greater control; and they have unleashed forces in the natural environment we neither fully comprehend nor direct. Students at Calvin should have a knowledge of the fundamental orders, processes, and histories of the natural world; they should grow in their awareness of the complex interrelationships of the delicate eco-system. They should gain insight into the way the natural world has been organized and transformed by human culture and its manifold technologies. In addition, they should gain a sense for the history, development, and contingency of the natural sciences, the philosophical assumptions of the naturalistic worldview, the nature and limits of scientific knowledge, the kinds of ethical questions that beset scientific research, the formative role science and technology play in our society, and the issues involved at the intersection of science, technology, and Christian faith.

VII. Human Society

Unique to human beings is the formation of domestic, social, economic, and political institutions by which human life is nurtured, human contact normed, the exchange of goods and services regulated, and the demands of justice sorted out. These institutions are both large scale and intimate, ranging from familial groupings to international organizations. Rightly constituted, they both condition and promote human flourishing. Ill-conceived, ill-formed, or ill-managed, they stifle the human spirit, perpetuate gross injustice, and occasion terrible conflict. Students at Calvin College, who are being trained for a life of Christian service in contemporary society, should gain a basic understanding of the institutions and social practices that shape North American culture — their principal aims, their origins and development, their mutual interaction, their global contexts, and their differentiation along such lines as religion, race, class, and gender. In addition, Calvin graduates should understand the basic concepts, theories, and methods of the sciences which study these practices and institutions, so that they may serve as wise agents of transformation and reconciliation in a society sorely in need of God's peace.

VIII. *The Arts*

Humans are interpretive beings, and they embody their sense of life in a variety of cultural forms: books and buildings, dance and drama, triptychs and TV, poems and paintings, films and friezes, music and mosaics. These products and activities embody the convictions and practices which members of a culture share, providing them, both individually and corporately, with a sense of identity and purpose before God. By the imagination we engage these convictions and practices through the mediation of line and color, movement and image, shape and sound. Exposure to such works can be enlightening and ennobling, or misleading and degrading. Whether we turn to the arts as an antidote to boredom, or in the passionate quest for meaning, we are in either case shaped by them through the powerful agent of the imagination. Students at Calvin College should be led to a serious and sensitive engagement with works of art in a full range of media and cultural forms, in their own tradition as well as other traditions, in both their native tongue and their second language. They should learn how to be astute interpreters of such works of interpretation, enabled to gain insight from them, developing a sense for what is worthy and what is base, so that they may grow in their understanding of life as God has given it to be lived. As a result of such broad engagements with the arts, they should also come to a deeper understanding of members of other cultures with whom they share creation.

IX. *Historical Development*

The varied movements within the world of culture, the forces of social change, the interaction between different societal domains, the effects — often unintended — of human actions, the power of past events over the present, the origins and development of ideas and institutions, the layers of continuity and discontinuity within a tradition — all belong to the domain of history and historical understand-

211

ing. Students at Calvin should be well acquainted with the basic contours of Western civilization in a global context and so come to possess a broad historical framework in which to situate and relate what they learn in other subjects. They should acquire an understanding of the particular forces that have shaped their world, the better to pursue their callings within it; and they should have some acquaintance with distant worlds, removed in time, in order to gain a critical perspective on their own. In addition, they should acquire some sophistication with regard to the rhetoric and particularity of historical narrative and become aware of the common uses and abuses of historical knowledge in the justification of claims in contemporary political disputes.

Knowledge of Ourselves

"We also need to know ourselves — our nature, gifts, and callings — as we engage this world."

*An Expanded Statement
of the Mission of Calvin College*

X. Our Identities

In coming to know God and the world which we inhabit, we come, at the same time, to know ourselves. For our identities, although based on individual differences, are largely shaped by our relationships. We are creatures made in the image of God; and as the divine life is transacted among three persons, so too our life is molded, lived out, and fulfilled in communities of persons. These communities are founded in and by God; they embrace the relationships we bear to our parents and siblings, to our neighbors, to our colleagues, to our fellow citizens, to all with whom we share God's world. These relationships, in turn, are structured in history by such institutions as the family, the church, the state, and the market — institutions which mutually condition each other and jointly express deep intuitions about the purpose of human life and its good. In addition, these relationships, so structured, constitute the social meaning of our contingent differences — our gender, race, ethnicity, class, and the like. As a result of their work in the core curriculum, students should come to a deeper understanding of themselves as image bearers of God, fallen in Adam and redeemed in Christ; as members of the Christian church universal; as products of a particular kind of tradition, home, and family life; as participants in the great democratic experiment of North American politics; as players in a mercurial market economy; as persons whose experience and action in the world has been deeply shaped by science and technology and whose imaginations and ideals have been affected by the media to which they have been exposed. In coming to know themselves and the specific characteristics of their identity and situation, students will acquire a deeper understanding of the particular shape of God's call to them and the proper contours of their response to it.

XI. Our Bodies

Human existence is an embodied existence. With the body we engage the world — we move, speak, love, play, write, and build. Calvin graduates should know about the several systems of the human body, the guidelines for wellness and proper nutrition, the principles of training for strength, flexibility, and endurance, the role of body-image in the formation of self-concept, the sources and management of stress, the symptoms of our common maladies, and the effects of alcohol and other drugs, so that they may be responsible stewards of the bodies God has given them and make sensible choices in matters of diet, physical activity, and medical care.

XII. Our Emotions

We are not only biological beings, but also affective ones, subject to widely varying, and sometimes deeply troubling, emotional states. Joy, sorrow, grief, love, desire, anger, fear, hate, contentment, and their cousins powerfully mold our lives and the lives of those around us. They inform our character and motivate our actions. They shape and are shaped by our relationships to others. They tell us — and sometimes surprise us — about what we believe and the things we value. At Calvin, students should gain some academically based insight into the emotions, their role in ethical formation and the spiritual life, their common disorders and their social and physiological bases, the guidelines for emotional health, and the assumptions of the major theories of human personality, so that they may come to understand their own feelings and behavior, and those of others, know how to deal with destructive emotions, and rightly sort out the issues of life in an age which tends to see all human problems as occasions for therapy.

XIII. Our Minds

Humans possess the wonderful capacity to know. Each waking moment they experience what Edmund Husserl called "the miracle of consciousness." Sensation, perception, memory, concept and language acquisition, and the manifold higher-order operations of the intellect are all components of human cognitive ability. Students at Calvin, learners all, should come to understand the nature and roles of these varied processes, their biological bases, the social conditions of their development, their variations, and their dysfunctions. Moreover, they should gain insight into how sin clouds the mind, expressing itself in systematic biases of human cognition, so that they might be more wary in their ways of knowing, more cautious in their claims to knowledge, and less credulous in their comportment with others.

XIV. Our Hearts

Human existence is not wholly contained within creation, but is gathered, directed, and ultimately related to the Creator, the governor and redeemer of all things. That gathering point of human existence is the heart, which we, as followers of Christ, offer to God as the summary of our life before him; that relationship is the domain of the spirit, which depends on God for its life. Because Calvin College is a Christian college, it has a deep and enduring investment in the spiritual well-being of its students and the community it serves through them. During their stay at Calvin, students should grow in their awareness of their deepest identities as members of a community called and covenanted by God; they should gain, as well, a deeper insight into the dynamics of the spiritual life — how the human spirit opens to the presence of God and why it so often closes down. They should also mature in a working knowledge of the spiritual disciplines, so that they may benefit in their relationship to God from the cumulative wisdom of the Christian tradition in matters of spiritual growth.

XV. Our Gifts and Callings

All human beings have received gifts from God in the form of talents, abilities, interests, passions, and opportunities. With these gifts comes the responsibility to use them in the service of the human community in ways that convey God's grace, truth, mercy, justice, and healing presence in Christ. For God did not give us these things that we might heap up fame and fortune for ourselves, but rather that we might play our unique part in a community of persons who depend on each other for what they need. In this way we participate in God's care for the world. Students at Calvin College should be given, in the course of the core curriculum, ample opportunity for discovering the gifts that God has bestowed upon them; they should become aware of how the sins of pride, envy, greed, and fear often twist and distort their self-perception, making it difficult to see clearly what God has fitted them for; they should also be provided with some guidance in the ways they might connect their gifts to human need in response to God's call to love their neighbors — for our calling is found, as Frederick Buechner once said, where our deep gladness and the world's deep hunger meet.

Core Skills

The following is a list of skills all students should acquire in the core curriculum of Calvin College. Some of these skills are essential for progress in their studies at Calvin; all of them will be useful as they pursue their callings in the world; many of them will be reinforced and elaborated within the curriculum of a major concentration or professional program.

The Skills of Reasoning

I. The General Art of Reasoning

In many ways the art of reasoning lies at the heart of the intellectual endeavor. It is, however, daily threatened by an invasive market culture that thrives on the manipulation of impulse and image, sensation and association. Moreover, it finds little support in the popular or political argument of our day, which more frequently provides us with examples of informal fallacies than models of valid inference. While made aware of the limitations of fallen human reason in the discovery and communication of truth, Calvin students should nonetheless become accomplished in the art of reasoning. Through instruction, encouragement, correction, and constant practice, they should become adept at picking out the central thesis of an argument and assessing its supporting evidence according to relevant standards, at distinguishing between deductive, inductive, and hypotheti-cal-deductive arguments — and knowing the rules of inference for each. They should be well aware of the tricky business of deriving causal claims from statistical correlations. They should be able to an-alyze matters, making subtle distinctions; they should be able to set matters in their larger contexts, making insightful connections. In addition, they should know not only how to assess the cogency of rea-soning on the part of others, but also how to construct arguments for their own positions, testing them to see if they should be held, and if so with what degree of confidence. With such skills, students can be-come active and qualified participants in the dialectic that leads to re-flective knowledge.

II. Quantitative and Empirical Reasoning

Not all Calvin students will pursue disciplines or professions that re-quire a high level of ability in mathematical analysis or the quantita-tive methods employed in empirical research. But they will all live in a society that has become, in the words of the AACU's *Integrity in the Col-lege Curriculum,* "bombarded by numbers." To operate in that society they must possess computational skills sufficient for the conduct of practical life. In addition to those basic skills, Calvin graduates should achieve a degree of sophistication in forms of quantitative and empirical reasoning that will enable them to understand and assess arguments given in the public square and the marketplace, argu-ments often and increasingly couched in numerical terms.

III. Cultural Discernment

One of the distinctive features of the Reformed tradition is its insis-tence that the deepest motives of the human heart are religious in na-ture and comprehensive in scope, and that our relation to God will therefore condition and direct the way we relate to our world, our neighbors, and ourselves. Moreover, the Reformed understanding of life in this regard holds that we cannot opt out of the religious relation. Whatever we love the most is in fact our god. If we do not serve the true God, we will serve an idol instead — and human life will be distorted as a result. Calvin graduates, schooled in this tradition, should become skilled at detecting the religious import of human life in its varied cultural expressions — its political manifestos, its art movements, its architecture, its technology, its markets, its myths and types, its blockbusters and bestsellers, its sit-coms and docu-dramas, its plays and poetry, its styles of worship, in what it preserves, what it forgets, and what it promotes at the moment. Further, Calvin graduates should be encouraged and trained to make use of such discernment in providing leadership for appropriate institutional and cultural change.

The Skills of Communication

IV. The Rhetoric of the Written Word

Fundamental to success in academic endeavors at the collegiate level is the ability to write expository prose that is clear, concise, vivid, and convincing. Such ability is also of crucial moment in professional and personal life, indeed, wherever understanding is to be achieved through written communication. Calvin graduates should be accomplished in the rhetoric of the written word, able to produce jargon-free prose that is freshly fitted both to subject matter and intended audience, in a style that sometimes delights even as it informs and persuades.

V. The Rhetoric of the Spoken Word

In democratic and republican societies before the advent of print media, spoken rhetoric was the key to a successful career in the public world. Of the seven liberal arts, it was in fact most prized by those preparing for the active life. Although the role of the spoken word is now diminished by the availability of the written word and the ubiquity of the image, it continues to be an important skill for educated people in positions of leadership. From the classroom lecture to the sermon, from the business presentation to the impromptu address given at the meeting of a neighborhood association, speech remains an irreplaceable medium of human communication. Students at Calvin should have training in the fundamentals of oral rhetoric, so that they may present their ideas and beliefs in the classroom, in the public square, in the church, in groups, and on the job in a manner both winsome and forceful.

VI. *The Rhetoric of the Image*

Recent advances in digital technology — computers, scanners, cameras, desktop publishing, graphic programs, presentation software, webpages, and the like — have placed in our hands powerful means of communication by way of the image. Although all students at Calvin need not be trained as visual artists, they should become acquainted with the basic principles and techniques of visual communication, applying these principles to their own expression in a variety of media, from the organization of typographical elements on a page, to the visual representation of data and information, to the effective and succinct use of image and symbol.

VII. *The Discipline of Reading*

With the accession of image-based media, the diminishing role of books as companions and consultants in life, and the frequent spoonfeeding of pre-digested ideas from textbooks in the schools, the discipline of reading among our incoming students has gone into steady decline. As one of our colleagues put it in a comment on the core curriculum, students often read their assignments with the same mental effort they devote to watching TV — the words wash over them, but leave little that is won only by the hard work of analysis. Calvin students should be challenged and taught how to read with care, precision, and a great deal of energy; how to detect the logical structure of prose intended to persuade; how to assimilate material embedded in prose intended to inform; how to identify and interpret tropes; how to spot an author's rhetorical strategies, shifts, and devices; and how to appreciate an author's use of genre conventions in the interest of conveying sense.

VIII. The Discipline of Listening

Listening is to the spoken word what reading is to the written word. Both should be active, not passive, operations of the mind. Listening with care and attention is a prerequisite to participation in productive dialogue, where the interlocutors speak to, and not past, each other. In the course of their studies at Calvin, students should be encouraged in the classroom to grow in the discipline of listening, so that they may not only express their ideas clearly, but do so in collaboration with others, and thus make human conversation generative of deeper insight and mutual understanding. Unlike reading, however, listening is not limited to the spoken word, but extends, by the bridge of pitch and rhythm, to music as well. Students should also have ample opportunity in Calvin's core curriculum to become more conversant and discerning in the special rhetoric of music, which has become, by means of the mass media, a powerful and pervasive agent in today's culture.

IX. The Discipline of Seeing

If we have become a society bombarded by numbers, we have also been drenched by images — in plaster, print, video, and the cinema; on

221

canvas, billboards, skateboards, T-shirts, letterheads, and the computer screen. A Calvin graduate should acquire an understanding of the ways in which images communicate, powerfully shaping our imaginations and self-understanding, the conventions that govern the use of images in different contexts, and the perceptions of life conveyed in the imagery that does so much of the work of instruction and persuasion in our media-saturated culture. They should come to learn that looking, too, is an art, and become alert, attentive, and discerning in their perception.

X. Competence in a Foreign Language

We share the world with members of several hundred distinct language groups. As members of that global community, Calvin graduates with a liberal arts degree should have a facility in at least one of those languages in addition to their own. A second language is a key that unlocks the door to the people, literature, history, outlook, and activities of another culture. Contact with another culture in its native language, in turn, represents an opportunity for a significant expansion of the self beyond the provincialities and limitations of its particular place and time. Although language instruction at Calvin will always involve more than the simple inculcation of linguistic techniques, its students should nonetheless receive thorough training in the skills of understanding, speaking, and writing in a foreign language, if that language is modern, or the skills of understanding and writing, if that language is ancient.

XI. The Art of Cross-Cultural Communication

We live in a world of many cultures. The North American continent, home to most of our students, has itself become culturally complex as a result of European colonization, the institution of slavery, policies of forced migration, the cumulative effects of immigration, the growth of international economic systems, and development in the technologies of travel and communication. To live a life of effective service in contemporary society, Calvin students should become skilled at cross-cultural communication, at understanding and making themselves understood to those outside their tribe. For some, this skill will include a competence in a foreign language — although such competence alone does not guarantee success in cross-cultural communication. For others, cross-cultural communication will be conducted in their native tongue with those who share the same language but belong to a different culture. Both forms depend upon the ability to read subtle cues, to see how the world looks from the standpoint of a different community of interpretation and experience, to distinguish between the deep and enduring principles of human morality and their situation-specific applications, to discern and, where feasible, to adapt graciously to the cultural expectations of others.

Technological Skills

XII. The Use of Information Technology

The computer has irreversibly shaped the ways in which we obtain, produce, retrieve, transfer, display, and analyze information. It is difficult to think of any area of life that has not been touched, for good or for ill, by the continuing revolution in information technology. Calvin students should become competent and confident users of available information technology, in full possession of the skills of word-processing, electronic communication, navigation in cyberspace, and of searching, filtering, and interpreting electronically available data.

Research Skills

XIII. The Art of Executing a Research Project

The conduct of research at the collegiate level demands skills of which many of our incoming students have only the foggiest notion. In the core curriculum, Calvin students should be thoroughly instructed in the art of academic research, both individual and collaborative: how to formulate a research plan; where to locate relevant sources; how to make use of new information technologies; how to distinguish between primary and secondary sources; how to evaluate secondary source material; how to do bibliographic research; how to collect and evaluate empirical data; how to make, track, and organize research notes; and how to present the results of such efforts as individuals or in groups according to the conventions of the relevant genre.

Physical Skills

XIV. The Exercise of the Body

For all the media attention given to physical fitness and appearance, many North Americans of middle age are amazingly out of shape. Aside from any aesthetic difficulties this may present to their fellows, or to themselves, this is cause for concern because physical health, besides being a good in itself, is a prerequisite for other activities we judge to be important — from taking care of the kids, to participating in the life of the church, to writing books. Obesity, high blood pressure, indigestion, fatigue, sore backs, and immobile joints all conspire to slow a person down, making it all the more difficult to "run the good race," either literally or figuratively. While at Calvin, students should develop skills in several sports and leisure activities that will serve them well in their college years and for a lifetime, God willing, of health and fitness.

Core Virtues

Moral formation has always been an important component of the tradition of liberal arts education. At Calvin, the liberal arts tradition is centered in the core curriculum, and radiates from there into the major concentrations, professional programs, and the educational programming of the Student Life Division. It seems fitting, then, that a statement on the moral aims of a Calvin education should be located in a document on the purposes of the core curriculum, even though the project of moral formation cannot be limited to core courses.

Many students arrive on Calvin's campus in a state of acute social anxiety, self-conscious about their appearance and personality, uneven in their intellectual preparation for college-level work, in some cases damaged by conflicts in their families or unwise choices made in high school. They come to Calvin eager for new experiences, new relationships, and for the credentials they need to fit into the professional world and thus secure a niche for themselves in a rapidly changing and confusing economic environment. Their concerns and aspirations are neither trivial nor insignificant. But the college hopes, in the course of the education it offers, to lift them above the tyranny of personal problems, beyond the clutches of the imperial self, into an expansive world that invites their best efforts on behalf of God's kingdom of truth, justice, and peace. It seeks to foster within them the committed heart of a servant as well as the critical eye of a prophet. It wants to equip them with the knowledge and skills required for a life of Christian service, and the inclination to live that life. In the following we attempt to name and describe traits that mark such a life. These are virtues we expect to be exercised in the Calvin community even as they are commended to a life in the world beyond its campus.

While a specification of the virtues we would want to foster in our students will have definite implications for the content of the core curriculum, it will also and especially be crucial for the pedagogies we employ in the teaching of core courses. Thus we venture, in this section, into questions of pedagogy. And with some justification. For core curriculum and core pedagogy together make up the whole of core education, and they should not be considered separately — an ideal curriculum wedded to inappropriate pedagogy will have little effect; solid pedagogy trapped in a bad curriculum will be, to a large degree, wasted effort.

Virtues are settled dispositions to feel and to act in certain ways. A compassionate person is inclined, as if by nature, to be moved by human suffering. A person in possession of the virtue of honesty has the disposition to tell the truth. Vices are also dispositions. A callous person, bearing within the breast a heart of stone, disregards the needs of others as a matter of habit. A person saddled with the vice of deceitfulness has the disposition to lie whenever lying seems convenient. A particular array of virtues and vices, taken together, makes up a person's character.

From its very inception in the Greco-Roman period, liberal arts education has sought not only to equip students with knowledge and skill, but also to shape their character on the basis of some shared conception of the good for human life. Isocrates, Quintilian, and Cicero were no sophists, for they were deeply concerned about the moral formation of their students even as they fitted them with the powers of rhetoric. When the program of liberal arts education was later appropriated by the Christian church, it was not divested of its moral import. But it was brought to a different understanding of the human condition and the moral project. In the Christian community, moral formation is not a matter simply of drawing out and directing the innate potentialities of human nature. For Christian doctrine teaches us that human nature has been deeply damaged by the power of sin, far beyond the repair of any human agency. To live aright, we stand in need of God's grace, God's forgiveness, and the enabling power of God's Spirit. The virtues we enjoy are not of our own making. They are the "fruits of the Spirit," the results of God's work with us (Galatians 5:22-23; Philippians 2:12-13). They are the family uniform of those who have died and risen with Christ (Colossians 3:1-4, 12-14).

This is not to say, however, that the acquisition of virtue is a wholly passive or mystical affair for the Christian. We are called to co-operate in this process of putting on the new person in Christ by shunning evil, by practicing the disciplines of prayer, confession, and fasting, by listening to God's word and participating in the sacraments. We are instructed to correct and reprove each other, to set and to follow good examples. We are, in short, to "train ourselves in godliness" (I Timothy 4:7). Christian liberal arts education, then, if it is true to its educational ideal as well as its religious roots, will also attempt to foster within its students the virtues constitutive of a life well lived, drawing its conception of the good life from the teachings of the Old and New Testaments, the example of Christ, the moral traditions of the church, and ethical reflection guided by the same.

Although CLAE *(Christian Liberal Arts Education)* was an attempt to spell out the meaning of the liberal arts ideal for a Christian college such as Calvin, it was curiously silent on such topics as the virtues and character formation. It is difficult to know how to account for this lacuna. Perhaps, at the time, that point was so well and pervasively understood that it seemed superfluous to make explicit comment on it. Perhaps it was assumed that character formation is the exclusive business of the church, or the Student Life Division. Perhaps Calvinist higher education to date has been overly intellectualistic, emphasizing the content of belief while ignoring the character of the believer. Perhaps it was thought that any attention to moral formation would play into the hands of the pietist wing of the Reformed community, giving an inward turn to the Christian impulse of a Calvin education.

Whatever the explanation may be, it is clearly time to retrieve this major component of the liberal arts ideal, attempt to articulate it for ourselves, and agree as a faculty upon its main contours. Most of us are the intellectual products of graduate programs in secular research universities, where education is ostensibly "value-free" and instruction attempts to maintain strict neutrality on the question of the good. We acquired a certain kind of knowledge; we acquired certain kinds of skills. What we would do with them, the kind of life we proposed to make with them, even how we acquired them, was our own business. Perhaps many of us have absorbed the ethos of neutrality in matters of education and therefore find it difficult to see what more teaching in the disciplines could possibly amount to. Perhaps we think that moral suasion is the business of RAs, not PhDs. But, of course, education has always amounted to more than the mere impartation of knowledge and skills. Even in the secular research university, certain virtues are being inculcated, a particular version of the good pursued, however implicit or unacknowledged. At a liberal arts college, we should be up front and intentional about the unavoidably formative effects of the educational process, and at a Christian college we are in an excellent position to do so.

Yet even though the virtues require our explicit attention, it is more likely that they are caught rather than taught — at least, if by teaching we mean the transfer of objective information and the like. There would be nothing quite so ridiculous, nothing that would elicit so much cynicism among our students, as a required course entitled "Virtue 101." Virtue, and its nurture in the souls of our students, then, will be primarily a matter of pedagogy. How are virtue and good character promoted in our teaching? Roughly: by exemplifying virtue in ways both admirable and worthy of imitation; and by inviting students to engage in those activities where virtue is both exercised and required for success. The virtue of courage, for instance, is inculcated not by teaching our students about the nature of courage but by inviting them to partake in those activities where courage is required. In the absence of a war, sports will usually do. It takes a lot of fortitude to dive into the fray of a soccer game, to slide into third base head first, to push through exhaustion while running cross country, to go in for a layup amid a thicket of elbows and knees. Likewise, there are difficult questions to be tackled in the classroom that often call for a great deal of intellectual courage. We can model courage in an academic setting by taking those questions on; we can foster courage in an academic setting by asking our students to do the same. A pedagogy that shapes character as well as it informs the mind is a pedagogy that provides good examples of the virtues it seeks to impart and invites students to be active in learning so that they may acquire those virtues for themselves. Intellectual character, and its moral analogs, cannot be developed on the sidelines of the academic life. Students must be encouraged to become participants, to get wholly involved in the project of shared inquiry, if they are to develop the kinds of dispositions that will make for a life well lived both within the academy and beyond its walls.

In the tradition of moral philosophy, the virtues are usually divided into the intellectual and the moral. This division should not give the impression, however, that they can be neatly separated in all respects. For the intellectual project, in reality, is a social endeavor. We chase after knowledge not in isolation, but in groups. If we do not exercise such moral virtues as charity, humility, honesty, and justice, we will obstruct the intellectual process of inquiry and impede the shared search for truth.

In the following list we name and describe those virtues we think play a special role in the life of the mind and the building of community, both at Calvin and in the world at large. The list is neither systematic nor exhaustive. It is, rather, exemplary, tailored to the mission of the college as an academic institution. Moreover, it does not seek to suggest, by describing the virtues under separate headings, that the virtues can be possessed in isolation from each other. Abstracted virtues quickly become vices: diligence becomes workaholism, honesty degenerates into brutality, and generosity slides into carelessness. The virtues must be mutually tempered and ultimately bound by the master virtue of love. As God's chosen people, we are enjoined by St. Paul to clothe ourselves with "compassion, kindness, humility, meekness, and patience," but above all to clothe ourselves "with love, which binds everything together in perfect harmony" (Colossians 3:12 and 14).

I. Diligence

The acquired habit of expending considerable energy in the steady pursuit of some goal, diligence is required wherever excellence is sought. It is the willingness to dig in for the long haul, to forego lesser goods in the present for the sake of greater goods in the future. It is grounded in the realization that "fine things are hard," and rooted in the hope that effort in the same direction over a long time will eventually yield results well worth the wait. It is the condition of real accomplishment in any field that requires more than luck and good fortune. In the academic life, it means not giving up on a difficult text when that text can't be understood the first time through; persevering with a problem until a solution is found; repeating the conjugation of a verb in a strange tongue until the proper endings become second nature. At Calvin, the academic workload should be gauged, pitched, and paced so that it is impossible for students to do well without exercising a great deal of this particular virtue. While no instructor should push students to the point of despair, no course at Calvin should be set up so that students can coast through it and still get decent marks. Calvin should be a place where students must get serious about their intellectual work if they are not already, learn how to manage their time, plan ahead, turn off the TV, and study even when they don't feel like it. The acquisition of such habits of diligence will stand them in good stead in their callings, whether they remain in the academy or venture beyond its walls. In addition, members of the faculty at Calvin should set a good example of this virtue in the classroom, investing considerable amounts of fresh and visible energy in their pedagogical efforts.

II. Patience

The virtue of patience is an essential support for the practice of diligence. Unfortunately, patience, like diligence, is not encouraged in our society, whose commercial culture runs on the engines of instant gratification. Patience is the ability to absorb a great deal of life's trouble — including pain, fatigue, setbacks, delays, annoyances, and the like — without loss of self-control, without caving in or blowing up. Students, in whom the private vice of impatience has been cultivated as a public virtue in the marketplace, should be coached and encouraged at Calvin to wait for results that can only be had after a long and sometimes difficult period of effort. They should be weaned from unrealistic expectations of instant and effortless success in their academic endeavors. The tasks assigned to them should, because of their difficulty or magnitude, require patience. Members of the faculty should therefore avoid devising occasions of cheap and easy success for the sake of making students feel good about themselves or the classes they take. Self-esteem in matters academic should be based on the reality of accomplishment, not the empty gestures of affirmation by instructors who think of themselves as therapists. Moreover, in our teaching we should not be given to quick and easy solutions where there are none, but be willing to do in the classroom the kind of patient work we expect of our students in their studies, ready to absorb a great deal of trouble for the sake of solid achievement.

III. Honesty

Intellectual honesty is often equated with the conscientious avoidance of plagiarism. Although honesty in matters of the intellect certainly includes truth in citation, it goes much deeper: it means not dismissing data, evidence, or argument in order to hang on to our favorite theories, not covering our eyes and stopping our ears in order to remain in our mental, moral, social, or religious comfort zones. An intellectually honest position is one that has given careful consideration to counter-veiling evidence; one that has fully explored and fairly assessed opposing arguments; one that has seriously contemplated alternative explanations and is able to state them with precision. Intellectual honesty can be fostered in our students by holding them accountable in their work for a careful consideration of viewpoints in opposition to their own, by not letting them get through the college without struggling with data, evidence, arguments, and views that might challenge the notions with which they entered its gates. Likewise, as faculty members, we should not allow ourselves to dismiss and ignore objections to our own positions, but be willing to show how we have dealt with them or — if they are new to us — display a willingness to review matters in a new light.

IV. Courage

As patience is to diligence, so courage is to honesty. It serves as an essential support. The intellectual landscape of our day is filled with formidable challenges, strange ideas, troubling issues, and unsettling questions. And the honest way though that landscape is not wide, straight, and smooth, but narrow, winding and rugged. Moreover, it is not always clear from the outset where the journey on that road will take us, what among our cherished belongings we will have to discard along the way, or how we will be changed as we make progress. Intellectual courage signifies the willingness to take risks, to take on the hard questions and follow the answers wherever they lead. It means relinquishing one's position when that position has been shown no longer to be tenable, as well as holding on to one's well-grounded convictions in the face of ridicule and hostility. Courage can be modeled in the classroom by asking the hard questions; changing one's mind when asked to do so by the evidence; and sticking to one's guns when conviction demands tenacity. Courage can be fostered by helping students to do the same. The college, moreover, can support this virtue by belaying and advising its more adventurous faculty members as they search out new and difficult routes on the previously un-explored faces of their disciplines.

V. Charity

In moments of intellectual conflict, disagreement, and exchange of opposing standpoints, it is tempting to caricature an opponent's position in order to dismiss it, to create a straw person that can be easily knocked down, to impute errant motives so as to make a position — whatever its content — look morally suspect and untenable. In the academic arena, charity is a matter of giving other people the benefit of the doubt, of putting the best face on their positions, of assuming their sincerity as seekers after truth. More generally, it means speaking and writing with clarity, so as not to confound or confuse others, listening attentively enough to be able to summarize accurately what someone has said, arguing without acrimony, being ready to praise what is genuinely praiseworthy in an otherwise faulty presentation. Students should be encouraged to practice charity in their academic work, granting those with whom they disagree a sympathetic hearing, giving a charitable interpretation to positions they may find strange or offensive, and treating others with respect, ever on the lookout for what is good within. Likewise, we should demonstrate this virtue in class when we are challenged by our students; when we are representing positions with which we strongly disagree; when we are moderating student discussions or commenting on their work.

VI. Creativity

Creativity is an excellence of the imagination. It is the springboard of the arts, suggesting new and arresting combinations of pitch and rhythm, of image and metaphor, of media and material, and new connections to the social context. But it is also the generative source of the sciences and the achievements of practical life. For scientific theories are not dictated by empirical data. They too are the products of the human imagination, even if they are subsequently tested and sorted out on the basis of empirical findings. Likewise, solutions to practical problems are not forced by circumstance, but invented by those whose minds freely range over a multitude of possibilities. Through their liberal arts education, students at Calvin should be encouraged to stretch their imaginations and find joy in the creative moment. For fresh expression in the arts, advances in the sciences, and new approaches to seemingly intractable problems of practical life all depend on the ability of the human mind to move from the actual to the possible and the willingness to take risks in realizing the latter. Moreover, at Calvin, students should come to discover — perhaps to their surprise — that the Christian faith can serve as a vibrant source of creativity, not a limit upon it, suggesting insights and approaches that are novel, striking, and largely unexplored in our secular age. This can readily happen when faculty members provide the example, ever on the lookout for the untried potentials of their faith as it bears on the issues and problems presented in their disciplines.

VII. Empathy

A deep and creative grasp of a subject requires empathy, an imaginative transposition of the whole self into the matters to be understood, a readiness to experience the world as others have experienced it. Whether it strives to comprehend a Greek tragedy, a medieval monastery, modernist architecture, or a secular ideology, the human mind comes to grasp more fully and more vividly what it can understand from an imaginative standpoint located at the productive center of the phenomenon in question. In our classroom instruction and exercises, with mature guidance and appropriate caution, students should be encouraged to move about in their imaginations, to inhabit locations that differ significantly from their own, standpoints from which the world not only looks different but feels different, so that they may be disposed to understand the works and words of those of different background and experience, those with a different temperament and sense of life, those of the opposite sex, those of a distant social stratum, those who have suffered what they have not, those who occupy a different historical world or subscribe to a different set of beliefs and attitudes — a Socrates, a Darwin, a Malcolm X, or a Simone de Beauvoir; in short, so that they may come to acquire an understanding of their culturally distant neighbors that is thoroughly enlivened by the powers of empathy.

VIII. Humility

In our academic pursuits we should strive to achieve a just estimation of our powers as finite and fallen knowers and thus come to possess the virtue of intellectual humility. To possess such a virtue is not to despair of knowledge or the truth. Humility is not skepticism, but a realization that our faculties are limited and fallible, that all cultures have their blind spots, and that we should therefore remain open — even as we carry on with our convictions — to correction by fresh evidence, new argument, and more experience. Humility before a text is grounded in the expectation that we will have something to learn from it; humility before experience, in the realization that experience is vast and ever instructive; humility before other persons, in the recognition that they are complex, varied, and inventive, and therefore may have something unexpected to say that will change our minds. We can exemplify this virtue in the classroom by readily admitting our noetic limitations and openly displaying a commitment to our own "continuing education," whether that education is to be found in the great texts and works of a tradition or the remarks of our students. Students, likewise, should be encouraged in the classroom to keep themselves open and teachable, even on matters they believe they have already sorted out.

IX. Stewardship

The world and all it contains has been entrusted by God to the care of the human race. We are to cultivate it, tend to it, learn from it, delight in it, develop its manifold potentials, and manage it in ways that benefit the entire human community and other living members of the bio-sphere. We are not to waste it, spoil it, or use it up for ourselves at the expense of others. Yet there are many forces in our culture that would prompt us to squander the time, talent, and resources that God has graciously placed at our disposal. We often treat our natural environment as if it were infinitely resilient; we sometimes spend our days as if we had all the time in the world; we discard our things as if there will always be more; we expend our energy on frivolous activities as if there will always be time for the important things later; we let our talents lie fallow as if there will always be someone else to take up the slack. The community at Calvin College should strive to set a good example in the wise management of time, talent, energy, and resources. Students at Calvin should become aware of the irreplaceable value of the gifts God has given them and the responsibilities attached to those gifts, and thus come to see themselves as stewards, not mere users, of the creation. Where appropriate, issues of stewardship should be addressed in our classrooms; where possible, students should be invited to participate in activities on and off campus that manifest care for God's creation — mending what is broken, cleaning what is soiled, nurturing the frail, conserving the scarce, saving the valuable.

X. Compassion

In a sermon on a passage from the book of Galatians, John Calvin once speculated that God could have created us as self-sufficient individuals, each inhabiting separate universes unto ourselves. That God did not do so, but made us creatures of needs that can be fulfilled only in human community, means that God intended his image bearers to live a life together in mutual love and service. Compassion motivates us to respond to the needs of others. It propels us beyond a self-centered and callous concern for our own interests into the lives of others, to promote their good and their welfare. It feels with those who suffer; it suffers with those who are in need. The social stratification of our society, the clean, well-lit places of our suburban homes, and the entertainment bias of the media have isolated us, mostly members of the middle class, from the suffering of others. The poor may be with us always, but we've done a pretty good job of hiding them. Life has been fairly sanitized, and we are insulated in many ways from the plight of our neighbors. Students at Calvin should find themselves, in their courses and their off-campus experiences, exposed to human suffering, invited into situations that normally elicit human compassion. They should be introduced, moreover, to lives that have been driven by compassion, to professionals who have not used their gifts and talents to shore up privilege for themselves, but have been quite intentional about directing their services and their resources to the benefit of those most in need of them. Likewise faculty members should reflect on whether their lives manifest compassion or whether the demands of success in their academic careers have narrowed their moral vision and blinded them in some respects to the needs of those around them.

XI. Justice

Justice is often emblazoned on the banners of the political left, while freedom serves as the watchword of the right. We often get the impression that we must choose between defending individual freedom, and letting social outcomes fall where they may, or promoting the cause of justice through the coercive power of the state, and leaving freedom by the wayside as a lesser good. Although there is an inescapable tension between these two ideals, they need not be posed as exclusive options. In order to protect the basic goods of human life, a community's commitment to justice will lead to legislation enforced by the sword of the state; but not all issues of equity can be handled in this way without violating basic freedoms. Thus even in a well-formed state there will be much to do in the name of justice. A personal commitment to justice is a commitment to use one's freedom to promote fairness in the way benefits and burdens are distributed in our society. Students at Calvin should learn about the principles of justice, the cases and causes of injustice in our society, both global and national; and they should be encouraged to form a commitment to the cause of justice, of doing what they can in personal, professional, and political life to insure fair treatment of all those who belong to the household of the human community. Likewise, a commitment to justice should be evident in the teaching we do at Calvin. It should govern the way we treat our students; it should have some bearing, where relevant, on the content of our courses; and it should list high among the concerns of the institution as evidenced by the speakers Calvin invites to its campus, the admissions and recruitment policies it pursues, the hospitality it extends to members of minority cultures and races, the service projects it sponsors, and the volunteer services it makes available.

XII. Faith

Faith, as a virtue, is the auspicious combination of loyalty and trust. To be faithful to another person is to remain devoted to that person, to keep promises made to that person, to share in advancing that person's legitimate ends. As such, faith is a feature of good marriages and friendships. To have faith in another person is to trust in that person's goodwill and competence, as when one has faith in one's physician. It is a prerequisite for learning from others, and thus of advancing in knowledge. Christian faith is found wherever ultimate loyalty and trust is directed to God through Christ. In every case, such faith is a gift of God's grace. For, as fallen creatures, we are inclined to be more devoted to ourselves than to God, more interested in advancing our own power and prestige than the purposes of God's Kingdom; and we are inclined to place ultimate trust in ourselves, or one of the

238

idols we have fashioned in God's stead. Christian faith comes when God in Christ makes it possible for us to repent of our sins, reach beyond ourselves, devote ourselves to Christ and his work of reconciliation, trust in him for our salvation, our guidance, and our care. But it also grows with exercise. As we experience God's goodness through faith, our faith is strengthened, preparing us for even greater demonstrations of God's goodness in our lives. Calvin should be a place where students find their faith nurtured, not only in chapel services and dorm Bible studies, but in the classrooms as well. In the core curriculum, students should find themselves reminded of the faith of those who have gone before them, in whose lives great things were accomplished through a childlike trust in God. The stories of God's people need to be told, and re-told. Students should also find evident faith in their professors, a faith that is deep, constant, and directive of their work in the classroom, their approach to the disciplines, their relationships to students and colleagues, and their bearing in the face of adversity.

XIII. Hope

Hope is the confidence we have in the realization of a future good we desire, either through our own efforts or the efforts of others on our behalf. As such, hope keeps us going in life. It's the spark that ignites our motivations. Without it we despair; in its absence we close up shop. On the other hand, it is possible for us to hope too much — to expect to bring about a good for ourselves that we cannot possibly obtain through our own efforts, as when a student might hope to ace an exam without so much as the slightest preparation. Such is presumption. To hope in ourselves for our ultimate good and happiness is human presumption par excellence, a product of our pride. In the end, we must admit our incapacities, and hope in God rather than ourselves. This kind of hope — Christian hope — requires faith, a complete trust in God's competence and goodwill, which has been demonstrated to us in the incarnation, life, death, and resurrection of

Jesus Christ. If we turn away from God, we will find ourselves sliding back and forth between presumption and despair. Only faith in God keeps us from presuming too much on our own behalf or despairing of the good we rightly desire for ourselves and others — eternal life in a world renewed in right relationships, in an everlasting city of justice and delight. Students at Calvin should find themselves enveloped in a community of hope that is both girded and guided by Christian faith. They should come to realize that the entire project of Christian education is premised on hope that is in turn based on trust in God's faithfulness to his people. They should come to see themselves as participants in the grand plan of redemption already vouchsafed in Christ, able to know real joy in their lives because of the hope that is within them. They should, moreover, learn to have a proper confidence in the gifts and abilities God has given them, recognizing that it is possible for them, with God's help, to make a genuine difference in this world. Equally, they should become acquainted with their own limitations, and thus learn not to presume beyond their abilities. Here the classroom can be of great assistance, providing feedback on students' efforts, assessing both strengths and weakness, abilities and limitations, so that they might serve well as "secondary agents" of transformation and renewal — secondary to the primary agency of God, for whom all things are possible.

XIV. Wisdom

Wisdom in practical life is a matter of pursuing ends proper to human life and making right judgments in the use of means in pursuit of those ends. It means, in effect, understanding how to live well and how the world works, so that the means we select are in fact conducive to our true ends. The wise build their houses upon the rock, because they know that sand is an unstable foundation. The foolish make traps into which they themselves fall — an unintended consequence. Those who possess wisdom have a keen sense for the ordering and point of God's creation — they have broken the color code of the

240

world's huge skein of wire; they know where the lines of causation and motivation begin, where they intersect, and where they end; they understand what it takes to get good results; and they realize that the good for human life is ultimately located in a right relationship with God. The foolish, on the other hand, stumble about in creation as if in a darkened room. They look for happiness in the wrong places. They get their wires crossed. They fail to achieve the right mix of measures, and find it hard to strike a balance in life; their actions are often inappropriate, ill-timed, ineffectual, or irrelevant. They frequently make things worse by trying to make them better, and wonder why. Although wisdom generally displays itself most vividly in an individual life, it is not an individual invention. Wisdom is developed over time in a tradition and carried in a community. It is communicated in proverbs, occasional advice, and apprenticeships; it is conveyed in the established patterns of a shared life. The tradition of Christian wisdom, which begins in a deep reverence for God, should be well represented at Calvin College. Students should find themselves being instructed in its ways in the classroom, the chapel, the dorm, on the athletic fields, throughout the halls, and in our offices. In addition, they should receive sound advice about Christian strategies for dealing with the ethical challenges they are likely to encounter in their personal and professional lives. At Calvin, a Christian college, they should find much evidence of the kind of wisdom that is more precious than silver, and learn to look for it as if it were gold.